The Life of Eva Perón

VICTORIA HADDOCK

The Life of Eva Perón

FIRST LADY, ACTIVIST, ACTRESS AND PHILANTHROPIST

VICTORIA HADDOCK

PEN & SWORD HISTORY
AN IMPRINT OF PEN & SWORD BOOKS LTD.
YORKSHIRE – PHILADELPHIA

First published in Great Britain in 2025 by
Pen & Sword History
An imprint of
Pen & Sword Books Ltd
Yorkshire - Philadelphia

ISBN 978 1 39908 032 3

A CIP catalogue record for this book is available from the British Library.

Typeset in INDIA by IMPEC eSolutions
Printed and bound in England by CPI Group (UK) Ltd, Croydon, CRO 4YY

The Publisher's authorised representative in the EU for product safety is Authorised Rep Compliance Ltd., Ground Floor, 71 Lower Baggot Street, Dublin D02 P593, Ireland.
www.arccompliance.com

For a complete list of Pen & Sword titles please contact:

PEN & SWORD BOOKS LIMITED
47 Church Street, Barnsley, South Yorkshire, S70 2AS, England
E-mail: enquiries@pen-and-sword.co.uk
Website: www.pen-and-sword.co.uk

or

PEN AND SWORD BOOKS
1950 Lawrence Rd, Havertown, PA 19083, USA
E-mail: uspen-and-sword@casematepublishers.com
Website: www.penandswordbooks.com

FSC www.fsc.org MIX Paper | Supporting responsible forestry FSC® C013604

Contents

Introduction

It is often said that tragedy gives rise to great myths, and nowhere is this more evident than in the short but meteoric rise of María Eva Duarte de Perón from childhood obscurity to influential stateswoman. No other modern historical figure has generated the number of complicated myths that she has. Her early death after only six years at the heart of Argentine politics fulfilled the tragic requirements needed to establish Evita as a legend of Argentina. For, 'As a First Lady, there had never been anything in Argentina like Eva … She was the New Woman, free and untrammelled.'[1]

Daughter. Sister. Actress. Wife. First Lady. Saint. Eva Perón's life was made up of a number of acts that saw an illegitimate little girl escape rural poverty to travel to the big city with dreams of becoming an actress, meet a presidential hopeful, and scale the heights of Argentine society to be known worldwide by the diminutive nickname 'Evita'. As the second wife of Juan Perón, she was able to advocate for women to get the right to vote, and her social aid programs helped many workers join the middle classes. Yet she would continue to be a polarising figure due to her often hypocritical nature and domination over Argentine politics. It could be said that during the early 1950s no other female in the world held as much power, thanks solely to her own talent and personality, as Evita. She achieved this status despite a personal life which directly challenged conventional Argentine society. The tough path she took to attain that power was one she preferred to screen from public view, but which both her admirers and detractors used to further their causes.

In her 1951 best-selling ghost-written autobiography, *La Razón de mi vida* (The Reason for My Life), Eva Perón wrote: 'Many persons cannot understand the circumstances which have made my life what it is. I myself have often pondered on all that is now my life.'[2] Growing up as the youngest of five siblings to a single-mother, clothing had a psychological impact on Eva. Her formative years rang out to the sound of her mother's Singer sewing machine, which brought in a much-needed income and clothed Eva and her siblings in homemade garments. The importance of the sewing machine in Eva's life later led to her giving away thousands of the machines through the Eva Perón Foundation, illustrating the transformative nature the sewing machine could have. It would be through her clothing, jewellery and hairstyle choices that Eva was able to transform herself from Eva Duarte to Eva Perón. She skilfully constructed her own image with a proficiency more akin to modern 'influencers'. Comparable to the constant style evolutions of Madonna (who famously portrayed Eva in the 1996 film adaptation of Andrew Lloyd Webber and Tim Rice's musical), Eva was aware from the beginning of how valuable an image could be, and even anticipated the image-focused social-media-absorbed world of the twenty-first century. Eva understood her physical appearance and how important it was to wear the correct dress for the right occasion (something that she learnt through trial and error). From her controversial entry into Argentine politics as the mistress of Colonel Juan Perón, she was aware that the media could be used to broadcast her chosen image, and her passion for the Argentine people, to the world. Fashion is sometimes viewed as something ephemeral, and even trivial, but it is something that is essential to all of us. Dress can transcend the person, while also identifying and reflecting them in a wider context. Eva was aware of the iconography that surrounded her style and set a high standard for future First Ladies.

This book will demonstrate that, aside from Eva's desire to appear fashionably dressed, there were a number of other factors that affected her clothing choices. During her lifetime, Eva Perón's wardrobe constituted a matter of state. Eva's adoption of haute couture was a direct challenge to the upper classes who resented her rise to the top, while also acting as a propaganda strategy for Perón's New Argentina. Eva's preoccupation with her image must also be understood in the larger social context of Argentina in the mid-twentieth century. Women were traditionally positioned in the role of devoted wife and mother (with motherhood often being viewed in the popular imagination as a journey to sainthood), or alternatively as a sinner or whore. By combining her active participation in politics with a 'fashionable' image, and the knowledge of how to dress well, Eva was able to demonstrate that social class and gender should be no barrier to the finer things in life. Eva would always claim that she spent money on couture gowns and jewellery for her loyal supporters, the *descamisados* ('shirtless ones') to inherit in the future. By showing that a small-town girl like herself could rise to the role of First Lady, Eva was perhaps Perón's greatest asset and physical representation of the benefits of Peronism.

While Eva's political career and life have been explored in multiple biographies, that often attest to her style and acknowledge the significance of fashion for the creation of her image, the significant role that Eva's personal dress played in her 'Cinderella' transformation in the public and political landscape has been largely overlooked. This book will aim to explore how and why Eva Perón chose to reinvent her image by using her clothing to inform and add to the biographical facts of her life. The intricate game of appearances in which she participated was where Eva felt more at ease. Her choice of colours, textures and silhouettes was the best weapon of communication available to her as a woman in the mid-twentieth century, and even though her style was admired and criticised alike, it continues to be the subject of much debate. To truly understand Eva Perón, and her mythical status, we must therefore start at the beginning.

Chapter 1

The Dressmaker's Daughter 1919 – 1935

The small agricultural town of Los Toldos, situated about 190 miles from Buenos Aires, was where Eva's story began. At the turn of the twentieth century, rancher Juan Duarte (born in 1872), a descendant of French Basque immigrants, left his wife Adela d'Huart and family in nearby Chivilcoy to manage the farmland of La Unión, Los Toldos, which he had leased with the prospect of making it a success. Duarte was popular among the Conservatives of Los Toldos, and his prestige saw him named Deputy Justice of the Peace in 1908. It was during his time in the area that he met Juana Ibarguren (born in 1894), the daughter of impoverished Spanish Basque immigrants. The couple became romantically involved, even though Juana knew that Juan could never gain a divorce from his wife due to the strict Catholicism which governed the country. In rural Argentina at that time it was not uncommon for wealthy men like Juan Duarte to have multiple families, and Juan and Juana's first child, Blanca, was born in 1908, followed by daughter Elisa in 1909, son Juan in 1911, Erminda in 1916, and finally María Eva in 1919. Eva's baptismal certificate lists the date of birth of Eva María Ibarguren as 7 May 1919. As the daughter of an unmarried couple, and a father who already had children with another wife, Eva was originally registered under her mother's surname. Eva's illegitimate status under Argentine law would haunt her for the rest of her life and be used against her time and again by her detractors and enemies.

When Eva was only a year old, Juan Duarte began to spend more time with his legal family, leaving Juana to raise their five children alone in Los Toldos. Despite some economic difficulties, Juan made sure that his second family were taken care of as best he could; biographer John Barnes noted that Duarte left a document declaring that the five children were his offspring and so were entitled to use the Duarte surname. As with any small town, most locals knew everybody else's business and Juan's abandonment of Juana to return to his other family would have led to Eva and her siblings receiving hostile looks from disapproving neighbours. There is no doubt that the shame of her illegitimacy greatly impacted Eva's decision to mould a new image once she was able to. The family's fairly stable existence came to a sudden end on 8 January 1926 when Juan Duarte was killed in a car accident in Chivilcoy. Eva was only 7 when her father died, and even though she had not seen him often, his absence was strongly felt. The funeral that followed has been the subject of much speculation. On stage and in film there is often an unpleasant scene at the church gates as Juana, a young Eva and her siblings are portrayed as being blocked from entering the church to pay their last respects to their father by his first wife, who did not want her husband's mistress and children at the ceremony. Both Blanca and Erminda denied this chain of events ever took place, stating that the two families had been aware of each other and had shared a cordial relationship. In reality, Juan Duarte had died a widower as Adela d'Huart had predeceased him, and therefore Juana viewed herself as Juan's widow. Dressed in black clothes that Juana made on her Singer sewing machine, the family travelled to Chivilcoy to say their final goodbyes to Juan. Without their father, who had always paid the rent and the bills, Eva and her siblings became even more aware of the stigma of illegitimacy that hung around the family.

Los Toldos had a reputation of being a deprived area, and without the means of support from Juan Duarte, Juana turned to sewing to provide for her family. She undertook a dressmaking course at the local school and earned a living by making clothes for neighbours and for a store that sent her patterns to assemble. Her daughters remembered hearing the repetitive clack of the pedal of the Singer sewing machine as Juana sat hunched over her machine for hours on end. Elisa and Blanca helped while also taking it in turns to care for their younger siblings. The long hours and hard work led to Juana developing varicose veins but she ignored her doctor's orders to rest her ulcerated legs as she knew that her sewing was the only thing keeping the family from starvation. The Duartes' dependence on the sewing machine was something that Eva never forgot, and Juana's sewing machine has since been saved and displayed in the Museo Provincial Casa Evita in Eva's childhood home. Without her father in her life, Eva's mother's income as a dressmaker not only kept the family fed, clean and healthy, but also allowed the family to keep up the appearance of respectability. The suffering and injustice that she witnessed growing up fuelled Eva's passion for social welfare. Writing in her autobiography, she would recount the impact of her mother's labour to support her children on her childhood: 'The mother of the family is left out of all security measures. She is the only worker in the world without a salary, or a guarantee, or limited working hours, or free Sundays, or holidays, or any rest.'[1]

In 1927 Blanca became the first of the Duarte siblings to leave home; she studied at the teacher training school in Bragado. Elisa began working at the local post office, and an 8-year-old Eva started attending primary school in Los Toldos. Schoolchildren in Argentina in the 1920s attended school wearing starched white smocks, which were meant to take the equalising form of uniform by concealing the student's clothes underneath. Juana was able to provide regularly cleaned and ironed smocks for her children but couldn't afford the leather brogues and 'Mary Jane' shoes worn by the wealthier pupils. Eva and her siblings instead wore canvas alpargatas (roped sole espadrilles), that marked them out as different and made them aware, from an early age, of their poor origins.

Eva's childhood in the town was mostly spent outdoors, or putting on plays, with her closest sibling, Erminda. Juana could not afford to buy toys and new clothes, so the Duarte siblings regularly made their own entertainment. Juana's passion for sewing was transferred to her daughters, who sometimes assisted their mother and made costumes for carnival. As the youngest of four girls, Eva usually swapped clothes with her sisters (a practice she maintained throughout her life). By making Pierrot and fairy costumes out of the inexpensive materials they had to hand, Eva and her siblings were allowed to transform themselves into whatever they wanted to be; the young Eva learnt that clothes had the power to create a character. Eva and her sisters would have been aware of the latest fashions through their mother's work and magazines of the period. It was said that Juana was able to provide her daughters with clothes every bit as fashionable as those purchased from a store with her trusty sewing machine.

In 1930, Juana moved her 'tribe', as she fondly called her family, to Junín. Elisa had recently been transferred to the city, situated sixty miles from Buenos Aires, with her job in the post office and quickly realised that the city would offer more prospects for the Duartes than Los Toldos ever could. The city was a big change to Los Toldos, with its stores and cinema, and would be the setting for Eva's formative years. The family took up residence in a one-room apartment. Juana supplemented her income from sewing by cooking in the houses of the local estancias to pay the rent, and Eva's older siblings soon became settled in employment in the city; Blanca returned to her family to take up a position as a teacher at the Sacred Heart School, and Juan worked as a salesman.

With Erminda starting secondary school at the Colegio Nacional, Eva's place as the youngest in the family became increasingly established. She was registered as a pupil at the Public School #1,

Catalina Larralt de Estrugamon. In time, owing to financial help from Elisa and Juan Jr., the family were able to move into a larger house, which Juana converted into a boarding house. Establishing herself as a respectable boarding house proprietor, Juana chose to swap her sewing machine for the stove. Noticing the lack of good restaurants in the city, she started to offer cooked meals for patrons. Two of her regular customers eventually became part of the family. Major Alfredo Arrieta, Commander of the 17th Military District, married Elisa in 1936, and lawyer Dr Justo José Alvarez Rodriguez wed Blanca. It was through the support of Justo's brother, Don José Alvarez Rodriguez, principal of the Colegio Nacional, that Eva would be allowed to pursue her dream of becoming a famous actress.

Like most teenage girls in the 1930s, Eva was an avid fan of the movies from the Golden Age of Hollywood and Argentine cinema. She regularly visited the cinema and absorbed herself in the popular film fan magazines of the period with their beautiful photographs and glamorous stories of the rags to riches lives of the stars. Borrowing and begging magazines from her friends allowed her to build up a scrapbook of her favourite images of stars such as Norma Shearer and Mary Pickford. These Cinderella success stories offered Eva a glimpse of the exciting world that existed beyond Junín and nurtured an ambition within her. A photograph taken of Eva aged 13, at home in Junín, shows a smiling, slim girl wearing a pink patterned cotton dress with a white piqué collar and cuffs. Until the day that she could emulate her favourite actresses and undertake a Cinderella transformation, Eva realised that she would need to develop a talent. Eva's dedication to her 'artistic vocation',[2] as she called it, led to her becoming known locally for her poetry recitals. Looking back on her childhood, Eva wrote in her autobiography: 'Even as a little girl I wanted to recite. It was as though I wished to say something to others, something important which I felt in my deepest heart.'[3] Whether it was due to the instability of her home life, or persistent absence from school, Eva never truly excelled in her education, but she did stand out in other ways. Eva's teachers recalled her entertaining the younger children with poems and songs, and it wasn't long before the childhood theatricals of her youth were replaced with roles on the stage.

When Erminda began secondary school, she became a member of The Commission of the Artistic and Cultural Centre of the Colegio Nacional, who assisted the students in producing plays. Even though Eva wasn't a member, Erminda was able to get her sister involved and Eva made her stage debut in a small role in the patriotic play *Arriba Estudiantes* (Students Arise) in October 1933. The positive experience reinforced Eva's determination to become a professional actress. It was also in Junín that Eva's voice was broadcast to the public for the first time, over loudspeakers installed outside the Primo Arini music shop. One evening a week, local youngsters were offered the chance to take control of a microphone and share their skills during the 'Hora Selecta'. Budding actress Eva chose to recite a repertoire of poems. These small encounters of fame made Eva realise that she didn't want to wait until she had finished her secondary school education to pursue her dream. Juana was adamant that Eva should finish school, and older sister Blanca later reminisced about the conflict Eva's ambition caused to the family:

> Even as a child, she had shown remarkable artistic talent. In the beginning we believed that her desire to be an actress was only a childhood dream. But her stubbornness in fighting for her dream led to lots of problems at home. Mother's opposition to Eva's dream was rooted in her desire to protect her child.[4]

Once Eva had made up her mind that she wanted more than the traditional married lives of her sisters, there was nothing stopping her. Eva described herself in *La Razón de mi vida*:

> Like the birds, I've always preferred the freedom of the forest. I haven't even been able to tolerate that minimum loss of freedom which comes from living with your parents or in your hometown. Very early in life I left my home and my hometown and since then I've always lived free. I've wanted to be on my own and I have been on my own.[5]

Eva entered competitions and requested auditions with radio stations, getting the odd part here and there. But she knew that to really have a chance of success she would need to leave Junín behind. Another myth that has grown up around Eva surrounds the circumstances in which she eventually left Junín for Buenos Aires. Andrew Lloyd Webber and Tim Rice's musical portrays a seductive Eva leaving for the capital with Tango singer Augustín Magaldi (1898–1938), referring to him as 'the first man to be of use to Eva Duarte'. Different narratives present Magaldi as either providing Eva with letters of introduction to radio stations in Buenos Aires, or mediating with Juana on Eva's behalf. Historians Marysa Navarro, Nicholas Fraser and Dolane J. Larson have found no record of Magaldi performing in Junín during the years that Eva lived there. It is more likely that Eva's dogged determination and constant pleading with her mother won out. Blanca remembered: 'No one could dissuade her. She showed the same iron will and determination which would mark her for the rest of her life. She insisted and insisted.'[6]

Valuable support for Eva's dream came from Don José Alvarez Rodriguez. As principal of the Colegio de Nacional de Junín, Alvarez Rodriguez had allowed Eva to act on the stage with the secondary school pupils and knew of her ambition from the conversation around Juana's dinner table. When Juana approached him for advice about allowing her daughter to live alone in the big city, Alvarez Rodriguez backed Eva. Having most probably seen many parents and children go through the same conflicts, he told Juana that she couldn't stand in the way of Eva's talent and that it was her duty to let her daughter at least try to make a success as an actress. Juana conceded defeat. Eva herself wrote that Juana chaperoned her to Buenos Aires, where the pair visited radio stations for auditions until one finally agreed to give Eva a slot on the airwaves. On the evening of 6 October 1934, Blanca, Elisa and Erminda were surprised to hear their younger sister's voice coming through the radio, reciting the Amado Nervo poem, *Where Do the Dead Go?* The director of the radio station was so impressed with the new talent that he offered Eva a short contract. To Juana's annoyance, the contract meant that Eva had to stay in Buenos Aires, and she returned alone to Junín, leaving the youngest member of her 'tribe' in the home of family friends.

Eva relished her newfound freedom in a city where no one knew her background and soon cast aside the little girl from Los Toldos and Junín. What she could never cast aside were the memories of her mother working night and day at the sewing machine to keep her family fed, the stigma of her illegitimacy, and the deep divide between rich and poor that had marked Eva throughout her childhood. Her anger at the injustices faced by the Duartes, and others like them, would smoulder until she met the man who would allow her the opportunity to right what she viewed as past wrongs. Her close friend, designer Paco Jamandreu, described in his book how, in January 1935, Eva packed her few items of clothing in her suitcase, and wearing a 'thousand times washed white blouse, with her little beret,'[7] pleated brown cotton skirt made by her mother, and white shoes inherited from her sister, she boarded the train to make the final move to Buenos Aires. The accuracy of this depiction is subject to debate, but it does tell us how important clothing – and the memories that a garment can instil – were to Eva. What we do know for certain is that she became one of the many jobbing actresses visiting the casting offices along Calle Corrientes – Buenos

Aires' answer to Broadway – looking for her big break. She returned to Junín only for family celebrations, and explored her new home with her brother, Juan, who was stationed in Buenos Aires after being drafted into the Army. Juana was only content after Elisa and her husband moved to the city in 1936.

Chapter 2

Stardom Beckons 1935 – 1944

The Buenos Aires of the 1930s was a buzzing, cosmopolitan metropolis, known as the 'Paris of South America' due to its wide boulevards, café culture, theatres and European architecture. The city even had the only overseas branch of the department store Harrods of London, which opened in 1914. The 1930s are known as the 'Infamous Decade' in Argentine history; Buenos Aires became crowded with migrants from the rural provinces and neighbouring countries ruined by the Great Depression. The decade was marked by mass unemployment and poverty in the capital, and shanty towns began to appear around Buenos Aires' industrial heartlands. Eva would have been aware of the social problems that arose between the largely bourgeoise population of Buenos Aires and the economic migrants who would eventually form the political roots of Peronism.

For Eva Duarte, the first problem to overcome was how to survive in the big city without any educational qualifications or connections. The thick skin she had developed growing up helped her brave the unrelenting job hunt in the offices of radio stations, journalists and magazine editors. The teenage Eva, with her bobbed brunette hair and large brown eyes, was particularly striking. It has been said that the whiter skin tone on her face was the result of a childhood accident when Eva knocked a pan of boiling water onto herself. She was able to use her looks to her advantage by working as a photographer's model for magazines such as *Vida Artistica* and began to see her face smiling back at her from the pages of magazines she had enjoyed as a girl. She was able to make ends meet and practise her craft by acting in small parts on the radio, never losing the rising inflexion at the end of her sentences which she would later use in her political speeches. A new stage in the evolution of Eva's style also began upon her arrival in Argentina's 'Big Apple'. She slowly started to change the way she dressed, purchasing suits and blouses second-hand in her favoured exaggerated feminine style, befitting of an aspiring actress trying to get her big break.

Eva joined the Compañía Argentina de Comedias (Argentine Comedy Company) in 1935 and made her professional stage debut on 28 March in a small role in a production of *La Señora de los Perez* at the Comedias Theatre. Her performance was well-received, with theatre critic Augusto Guibourg writing in his review in *Crítica*, 'Eva Duarte was very good in her small part'. She was not always lucky enough to have her name mentioned in reviews, but she chose to stay with the Company, playing bit parts in productions such as *Mme. San Gene*, until January 1936. Throughout 1936 she toured nationally with a theatre company founded by the actors Pepita Muñoz, José Franco and Eloy Alvarez. In December 1936 she joined the cast of Pablo Suero's *Los Inocentes*, a Spanish translation of Lillian Hellman's controversial play *The Children's Hour*. Staged at the Theatre Corrientes in Buenos Aires, Eva Durante (as she is referred to incorrectly in the theatre programme[1]) was cast in the featured role of one of the schoolgirls, Catalina/Catherine. She was given the opportunity to travel abroad for the first time with the company to perform for a few days in Uruguay. Eva was then offered the chance to join the company of renowned theatre producer Armando Discépolo to star in La Nueva Colonia that opened at the Politeama Theatre in March 1937. Despite good reviews, including Augusto Guibourg's *Crítica* review that namechecked Eva as having 'acted gracefully,' the play was a box office flop.

Eva didn't allow failure to hold her back, and in 1937 her professional life changed for ever. She obtained a film contract to star on the big screen for the first time in the comedy, *¡Segundos afuera!* Directed by Israel Chas de Cruz and Alberto Etchebehere, and filmed in Buenos Aires, the film gave Eva her first taste of something she had dreamed about back in Junín: life as a film star. At the same time, she was also offered a contract by Radio Belgrano to star in their radio theatre drama, *Oro Blanco*. The opportunity she had worked so hard for allowed Eva to draw on her life experience and carve out a career conveying emotion in radio soap operas. As around every third Argentine household had radio access in 1937, radio roles in the 1930s were much more significant as they connected with a mass audience. The fact that Eva Duarte could rise to become Santa Evita in the hearts and minds of so many Argentines rests above all on her origins in radio.

As she entered her eighteenth year, Eva's star was finally in the ascendant, and in the following years she would act simultaneously on stage, in film and on the radio. As is customary with any young actress beginning to be noticed, Eva gained media exposure. She understood the importance a photograph could have in disseminating her image and winning future roles, and chose to be photographed by studios that specialised in taking portraits of actors. Eva was photographed by some of the leading photographers in Argentina at the time, including Polish-born Sivul Wilenski and German-born Annemarie Heinrich. She appeared on the covers of popular magazines of the time such as *Sintonía* in October 1939, *Cine Argentino*, and *Damas y Damitas* in December 1939. Vera Pichel, the editorial secretary of *Damas y Damitas*, recalled how Eva approached her asking for a promotional photograph. When Pichel offered to get Eva an interview with the director of the magazine, Eva forthrightly told Pichel that only a fellow working-woman such as herself could understand how Eva needed a photograph in order to work, and that she did not want anything to do with the director. Whether this reluctance to speak with the male director was due to the 'casting couch' phenomenon of the period is open to debate. The resulting cover photograph was taken at Wilenski's studio and shows Eva wearing a white terry cloth jacket and shorts with embroidered pockets and a striped belt. Eva improvised a blouse with a blue scarf. Her publicity shots taken between 1937 and 1940 alternated between modest portraits presenting her as a typical starlet, playfully posing wearing the latest fashions, and the risqué half-nude pin-up photographs that would not be publicised by Perón's government but would later be distributed by Eva's political opponents. One of the most famous of these, that Madonna would go on to recreate in the 1996 film Evita, is Annemarie Heinrich's photograph of Eva posing in a polka dot swimsuit that was published in *Unión* magazine in January 1940. Recalling the session where this image was created, Heinrich remembered; 'They asked me to take "good pictures and a little sexy, if possible", something I couldn't do because Eva wasn't sexy. She was a girl from the interior, very modest and simple.'[2]

Between 1938 and 1940 Eva continued to appear on the stage with a number of theatre companies. In 1940, she was cast in a supporting role in *La carga de los Valientes*. The historical drama film was one of the most expensive productions ever made in Argentina at the time, and told the story of the 1827 defence of an Argentine naval base during the Argentine-Brazilian War. Eva achieved some personal publicity upon the release of the film and daring photographs taken by Sivul Wilenski of her posed seductively with just a piece of material to cover her modesty were featured in the July 1940 edition of *Cine Argentino*. The text that accompanied the photographs highlighted Eva's ambition for stardom:

> She is young and beautiful. She has a definite temperament that, together with her photogenic faculties, can bring us one of the actresses of the new cinema hour. She is very interested in acting in theatre, but confesses that cinema has, for her, a

> powerful attraction, and that, in this sense, she feels strong enough to deserve a position.

Two more film roles followed, in the comedy films *El más infeliz del pueblo* (1941) and *Una novia en apuros* (1942), the first Argentine film to be directed by an American director.

Eva Duarte managed to achieve the impossible in the Buenos Aires of the 1930s and early 1940s: relative success as an actress and burgeoning fame. Her critics have cited this achievement as proof of Eva's unsuitability to be First Lady, for how could an illegitimate girl from the country accomplish having her photographs in magazines, her voice on the radio, and her face on the big screen in just a few short years? Many refused to believe that Eva's burning ambition and force of personality alone could have led to her conquering Buenos Aires and making powerful friends. Among her admirers were Colonel Imbert, the Minister of Communications, who oversaw radio in Argentina. Once she began a relationship with Juan Perón, gossip quickly began to spread that Eva must have slept her way up the social ladder in order to further her career. How on earth could an unchaperoned young woman have survived in the dangerous world of men? These misogynistic rumours were mainly shared by men, who perhaps found it hard to believe that a woman such as Eva had learnt how to play the game to become a star. She frequented the offices of *Sintonía* to spend time with the handsome editor, and racing car driver, Emilio Kartulovich. While waiting for him, she would sit and chat to the journalists, which resulted in her name being linked to that of Kartulovich in the gossip columns. Eva realised that just the suggestion of a relationship with powerful men in the business could gain her publicity and ultimately further her career. Whether sexual favours were employed we may never know. What many of her detractors didn't realise is that Eva was not alone in Buenos Aires. Her older brother Juan, who would remain a lifelong confidant, was also in the city and surely would have reported back to his anxious mother any transgressions on Eva's part. The fact that Eva put her career first in a society that positioned women as wives and mothers was viewed suspiciously by her enemies, who didn't understand that Eva's career was fuelled by her desire to transform, and to rise above her illegitimate status.

Eva could be described as the ideal modern woman of the early 1940s. She was much too invested in her career and in making her own money to think about sacrificing everything she had worked for to marry and support a family. The world of entertainment that she inhabited was viewed by outsiders as one of loose morals and therefore unacceptable for honourable women. The household chores such as washing and sewing, undertaken by Juana to support her family, and community service were deemed the only appropriate forms of employment for respectable Argentine women – mainly because they were considered beneath the role of men or extensions of the home, which was the woman's domain. By the mid-1930s, tensions had arisen between the different spheres occupied by women as traditional roles began to deteriorate. The social condemnation which Eva was subjected to arose from the feminine stereotype that placed women as mothers and wives. Eva challenged these domestic norms by choosing to leave her family in search of work, and by publicly displaying herself as an actress and model.

In 1942, Eva was hired by a company called Candilejas to co-star in their radio soap opera *Muy Bien*, which aired daily on Radio El Mundo. Curiously, the production was sponsored by a soap manufacturer who employed Eva's brother Juan. It is possibly just coincidence that Eva's own Cinderella life story mirrored that of the radio soap opera that made her a household name. Biographers Fraser and Navarro described Argentine soap operas as:

> the vehicles of their provincial audience's fantasies, the heroines were always young, always poor and obscure,

> always hopelessly in love with men beyond their station, and always chaste ... They suffered endlessly and then they were rewarded. Eva was good at conveying suffering. When she found the soaps she found her acting career.[3]

Years later, in an interview with *Antena* magazine, Eva praised the support of Radical Soap in furthering her career: 'I am delighted to act for a firm such as Radical Soap, which eight years ago, on Radio Prieto, gave me one of the first opportunities of my life, when no one believed in me and I was little less than a stranger.'[4]

Later that year she went on sign a five-year contract with Radio Belgrano, who had the highest audience nationally. The station's owner, Jaime Yankelevich, pioneered the use of contracts for his radio artists, in which they received a salary in exchange for the exclusivity of their output. This practice led to Radio Belgrano becoming the most coveted employer in Argentine radio. Eva's new role was in a historical drama series in which she played the roles of great women from history, including Catherine the Great, Queen Elizabeth I and Sarah Bernhardt. Broadcast daily in a prime-time evening slot from October 1943, the programme was another case of life imitating art, as Eva would soon go on to meet Juan Perón and begin her ascent to iconic status. In a 7 April 1945 interview in *Radiolandia* magazine, Eva reminisced about her radio career:

> I was lucky to go from one microphone to the next until I came to the one which for me is the best radio has to offer. In Radio Belgrano I found people who believed in my possibilities. Here I have reached the height of my career, a very rewarding career which began modestly but grew as I dedicated myself to my work, as I strove to perfect myself and to assimilate the very valuable lessons I received.

Eva would eventually come to co-own Radio Belgrano.

These roles gave Eva not only her first real taste of fame, but also financial stability, and she became one of the highest paid radio actresses in the country, earning between 5–6,000 pesos a month (£11,560–13,960 today). In 1942, she purchased an apartment on 1567 Calle Posadas in the exclusive upper-class Buenos Aires neighbourhood of Recoleta. Following her new roles, Eva was advised by studio hairdresser Julio Alcaraz to bleach her naturally dark hair blonde. Whether or not she was inspired by the glamour of American actresses such as Lana Turner, this makeover created an image that Eva would maintain for the rest of her life – and which would distinguish her from her peers, transforming the girl from the pampas into the image of the Hollywood actresses she loved. In the South America of the 1940s, going blonde represented a chance for social improvement. Alcaraz would continue to colour and style Eva's trademark hair, visiting the presidential residence every day, until her death. She began to favour elaborate rolled hairstyles worn together with brightly coloured and tightly fitting dresses. Her new look was disseminated to the public by studio portraits that she had delivered to the press. Eva was never egotistical enough to view herself as a great actress, and once told her priest and advisor, Father Hernán Benítez, that her acting skills had been 'bad in the cinema, mediocre on the stage, and passable on the radio'.[5] But what she could do was rouse an audience, a skill she would use to great advantage as First Lady. By 1943, Eva was at the top of her profession. Her image transformation into a blonde film star allowed her to present herself as a style icon and object of desire, like those she had looked up to as a child. This new look also allowed Eva to find a footing in the world of politics. She was already well and truly aware of the importance of spectacle and used her knowledge of the media to her advantage in order to present herself as a fashionable but caring woman onto whom people could project their needs. She made her first foray into politics that year as a founding member of the Argentine Radio Syndicate (ARA), a union for radio performers. She would be elected president by her colleagues in May 1944.

In a 1948 *Macleans* article titled 'She Dictates to the Dictator', Ray Josephs summed up Eva's acting career by stating: 'One eye was always on a leading lady's role that always seemed out of her grasp.'[6] But in January 1944, this was all about to change.

Chapter 3

Along Came Perón 1944 – 1946

On the evening of the 15 January 1944 a huge earthquake struck the city of San Juan, in the west of Argentina. Over 10,000 people were killed and 90 per cent of the city's buildings were destroyed. The organisation of relief efforts for the victims rested on the shoulders of the Secretary of Labour and Social Security, Colonel Juan Domingo Perón.

Perón was born on 8 October 1895 in Buenos Aires Province to rancher Mario Tomás Perón and Juana Sosa Toledo. Juan Perón's upbringing shared many similarities with Eva's. His parents also weren't married when he was born (they would eventually wed in 1901, with Mario acknowledging the legitimacy of both of his sons with Juana), and while the Perón family hailed from Spain and had enjoyed financial and social success in Argentina, he carried the stigma of his mother's indigenous ancestry. After attending boarding school in Buenos Aires, on the wishes of his paternal grandmother, 16-year-old Juan entered the National Military College to become an officer in the Argentine Army. At 6-foot-tall and strongly built, Perón excelled at boxing and fencing, and upon graduation progressed through the ranks. He joined the Sargento Cabral Military School as an instructor in 1920, where he wrote a number of chapters for the army's *Applicant's Manual*, which would become his first published work. By 1925, Perón had been promoted to Commander of the First Company of Infantry and had also met the woman who would become his first wife. Aurelia Tizón, or 'Pototá' (a play on the word 'precious') as Juan affectionately called her, was a teacher from Buenos Aires. Perón's junior, Aurelia, was highly cultured and encouraged Perón to look outside the machismo world of the military. The couple were married in a private ceremony on 5 January 1929, marked by the groom's mourning for his father who had passed away in November 1928. The wedding was one of the final times that Juan would see his mother and brother and he would have little contact with them for the rest of his life.

In 1930 Perón gained his first experience of political intrigue when he was invited by supporters of General José Félix Uriburu to join a military coup against President Hipólito Yrigoyen, who was struggling with the economic crisis caused by the Great Depression. While Perón liked Uriburu, he didn't trust that the general had any real clear support, and he also struggled with where to place his loyalty as he had previously voted for Yrigoyen in presidential elections. The coup took place on 6 September and marked the beginning of the thirteen-year Infamous Decade in Argentinean politics. Perón would later come to regret his role in the plot, stating that many members of the military collaborated only because they were following orders from their superiors. In the new provisional government of President Uriburu, Perón was promoted to the rank of major and joined the faculty of the Superior War School in 1931 as a teacher of military history. Between 1936 and 1938 he left his teaching position to serve as a military attaché in the Argentine Embassy in Chile. His diplomatic career was interrupted when Aurelia was diagnosed with cervical cancer (the same cancer that would also kill his second wife). Perón rushed back to Buenos Aires to be by her side when she died on 10 September 1938. As nearly all cases of cervical cancer are caused by the sexually transmitted Human Papilloma Virus, it is possible that Perón unwittingly caused the deaths of both Aurelia and Eva.

Still recovering from the loss of his wife a year later, Perón was assigned a new post by the Argentine War Ministry. An accomplished skier, he was sent to study mountain warfare in the Italian Alps. During his time in Europe Perón also served as a military attaché in

Rome and Berlin, where he was able to study the Fascist governments of Benito Mussolini and Adolf Hitler first hand. He returned to Argentina in 1941 and was appointed to colonel the following year. In 1943, Perón was one of the original nineteen officers to join the Army's nationalist secret society, the Grupo de Oficiales Unidos (United Officers' Group). He later wrote that he promoted the importance of trade unions and the rights of workers with his fellow officers, so that social changes could be implemented in advance of the military coup that the GOU were planning to overthrow the civilian conservative government of President Ramón Castillo. Castillo had been fraudulently elected to the office of vice president before he succeeded to the presidency in 1942, and the Revolution of '43 that took place on 4 June 1943 ended the electoral fraud of the Infamous Decade. Under the presidency of General Pedro Ramírez, Juan Perón first served as an assistant to the Secretary of War before becoming the head of the Department of Labour. It was in this inconsequential role that Perón would enhance his power in the military government, while also expanding his support network in the workers' movement (the same *descamisados* who would ultimately go on to vote him president in 1946). He promoted labour laws and improved working conditions by passing a range of social reforms that brought him into alliance with leaders within the Argentine labour unions. By December 1943, Perón was able to have the Department of Labour elevated to a cabinet-level office, and himself promoted to the newly established role of Secretary of Labour and Social Security.

The San Juan earthquake afforded Perón national prominence and public approval as President Ramírez entrusted him with the fundraising efforts. He was the first member of the government to address the country about the disaster, committing the nation to delivering urgent aid to the victims and to the reconstruction of San Juan. Perón adopted the radio as a major source of communication with the public and was able to galvanise the population in a way not seen before. For the first time, many women felt that Perón was including them as citizens who could make a difference by donating money or giving blood. He rallied celebrities and public figures to offer their support to the relief efforts – including Eva Duarte, who helped collect funds. The week of fundraising culminated in a benefit gala held at Luna Park on 22 January 1944.

One of the biggest myths surrounding Eva concerns her first meeting with Juan Perón. She may have already been acquainted with the colonel through her radio work or fundraising efforts, but most historians believe that it was the night of the gala that changed her life for ever. Some historians have speculated that Eva and Perón's mutual friend Colonel Imbert may have engineered the seat for Eva next to Perón that evening. Eva told a different story. Spying an empty seat next to Colonel Perón in the VIP area of the arena, she tried to get closer to catch his attention. She later admitted to her friend Vera Pichel:

> I don't know how I dared to do it. I didn't think about it, because if I had I would have stayed where I was … but the impulse did it all. I saw the empty seat and ran towards it without thinking whether it suited me or not.[1]

Both must have been aware that this meeting wasn't by chance, but Perón was fascinated by the confident, glamorous woman at his side. Eva and Perón discovered that they were united not only by a sexual attraction, but also a shared ambition for power. Despite the twenty-four-year age gap the pair struck up an easy conversation that lasted for over an hour. At the end of the show, Perón invited Eva to dinner, along with his colleague Colonel Imbert and his actress date. That evening Eva left the arena on the arm of Perón as the couples travelled to a restaurant in the Barrio Norte district of Buenos Aires. They spent the dinner talking as if they had known each other all their lives, so much so that they only realised they were alone when the staff had cleaned and closed up the restaurant around them. From there they moved to Perón's apartment at 3291 Arenales Street in the Palermo neighbourhood of the city. Eva spent Saturday evening, all day Sunday and part of Monday in Perón's apartment before being driven to Radio Belgrano in the evening in a chauffeured War Ministry car. Eva admitted to curious friends that the colonel was a strong and tender lover.

It was obvious to all who saw them that there was a spark between the new couple. Over the following weeks, Eva and Perón became inseparable. The colonel was impressed by Eva's radio career and, sensing how useful it could be to his ambitions, visited Eva at the studios of Radio Belgrano on 3 February 1944, with the resulting meeting being captured for posterity in what would be the first official photograph of the couple together. The image of a slightly coy Eva and Perón was published in *Radiolandia* magazine two days later. This very public announcement of their relationship added fuel to the fire of Perón's opponents from within the military who were critical of his blossoming affair with a lowly actress. Members of the military were shocked that Eva's career was actually benefiting from her association with Perón.

In May 1944, it was announced that broadcast performers must unionise in order to continue working. As the idea for a single union had come from Perón, unsurprisingly the other performers chose to elect his mistress as the first president. Taking advantage of her success, Eva began a new thinly veiled propaganda programme called *Toward a Better Future*, in which she extolled the 4 June Revolution and the actions of Juan Perón. This was not how things were done within the machismo culture of Argentina's military. Liaisons with actresses, while not accepted, would be tolerated if they were conducted clandestinely. Eva's presence at the side of Perón was unacceptable. Not only was Perón setting a bad example to his army colleagues for allowing his mistress this liberty, but many also began to become suspicious around Eva's motives. In response to the criticism Perón is purported to have said: 'They reproach me for going with an actress. What do they want me to do? Go with an actor?' Oblivious to the society gossip surrounding the couple's unmarried status, Eva took the opportunity to cement the future of her relationship when she spotted an apartment for sale next to her own on Posadas Street. She was able to convince Perón to purchase it, and they moved in together in April. The Catholic patriarchal society was affronted by the fact that a member of the government, and a military man, was living in sin by choice with an actress. Eva's public image and modern ideas were perceived as a threat to the social norms that dictated society in the 1940s.

The evolution from Eva Duarte the actress to Eva Perón the political spouse began from the moment the couple left the Luna Park benefit together. Her love life and rising career had not only brought her increased fame and a semblance of power, but also into conflict with the military and upper classes in Argentina, who resented her success and considered her vulgar. It was then that Eva Duarte decided to create some legitimacy to her new public position, by using fashion to cultivate a more sophisticated image. 'I'm going to defeat them on their own turf,' she said. The style of the time replicated the chic dresses and suits worn by American women, and as Buenos Aires in the 1940s was home to a number of haute couture fashion houses, such as Paquin, Eva should have had her choice of designers to help transform her. Unfortunately, her attempts to imitate the dress of the bourgeoisie that she so despised opened her up to further criticism as an upstart, and many designers turned their backs on associating with her for fear of losing their clientele. Slowly but surely, she began to remove any traces of the aspiring actress in favour of a more formal image. The new Eva meant business, and this was represented by the photograph in the 1 June 1944 edition of *Antena*, which showed her standing with her arms crossed, wearing a Paco Jamandreu[2] tailored jacket that would come to characterise her image as First Lady.

Paco Jamandreu, known as Paquito, was Eva's first couturier. While many of the Argentine fashion houses copied the designs from Paris, Jamandreu created a new silhouette for Argentine women that caught Eva's attention. Her first phone call to the designer was dismissed by Jamandreu, who did not consider Eva to be on a par with the film actresses and local elite that were his clientele. It was actress Nélida Bilbao who convinced Paco that meeting Eva could be beneficial to both parties. For that reason, Paco found himself at Eva and Perón's apartment one Saturday evening in April 1944. Paco wrote in his memoirs[3] of the impression he formed of the young blonde woman who opened the door, wearing a combination of a blouse, satin trousers and cork platform heels that he thought was in bad taste. Eva wasted no time in telling Paco why she had contacted him:

> I saw your drawings in *Mundo Argentina*. I like them very much. Now I am going to need clothes for my work as an actress, do you understand me, in radio and in cinema. You have to create a style for me. Because I'm going to make movies, you know? On the other hand, I need sport clothes, street clothes, very simple clothes for my work with the colonel. You can imagine; rallies, collections, visits to the slums, to the hospitals.[4]

After a tour of Eva's wardrobes – which Jamandreu quickly dismissed as tacky and out of fashion – the designer was introduced to Juan Perón. With her lover by her side, Eva got down to business by setting out her plans for working with Paco:

> Don't think of me as just one more of your clients. From now on, I will have a double personality: on one hand, the actress – there you can be as extravagant as you like with lamé, feathers, sequins. On the other hand, this bossy guy wants to make a

> political figure out of me. And we begin on May first. I have to go with him to a huge concentration of workers, people will gossip like mad, it will be the first appearance of the Duarte-Perón couple. What are you going to make for me to wear?[5]

'A suit,' Paco replied. The double-breasted houndstooth suit with velvet collar become Eva's uniform, her second skin, for mediating between the people and the government. As both Eva and Paco worked in the film industry, they were aware of the messages that dress could convey. Designed by Jamandreu, and possibly made by her future personal tailor Luis D'Agostino, the simple suit was a costume for Eva's transformation into Eva Perón.

Eva trusted Paco's style advice and even though she didn't exclusively wear his designs throughout her life, he would continue to mentor her on what to wear. Paco and Eva's relationship was initially that of designer and client, but quickly developed into one of candid friendship that impacted both their careers. Jamandreu was gay and often fell afoul of the laws on homosexuality in Argentina, which resulted in Eva driving through the night to pick him up from the police station. She also took him out of his comfort zone by having him accompany her on visits to the more deprived parts of Buenos Aires. Here, he witnessed first-hand Eva's charitable nature as she went among the people asking questions and handing out toys to the children. Recognised by some of the poor women, she told them: 'Write to me on the radio and ask for what you need. I'm not rich, but I will be able to do something.'[6] Eva also requested an evening dress from Jamandreu to wear to the gala at the Colón Opera House to celebrate Argentina's Independence Day in 1944. Eva and Perón would sit in neighbouring boxes, but the pure fact that a government minister would display his mistress so publicly was bound to raise eyebrows. The colonel wished to see Eva dressed like a princess, but Paco had other ideas. He designed a floor-length black silk dress with a bodice constructed from strips of black velvet ribbon over a nude silk gauze lining. Perón loved the daring design so much that he encouraged Eva to be photographed for *El Hogar* magazine, and also by Annemarie Heinrich, with the resulting image making the cover of the 15 February 1945 edition of *Antena*.[7] A new Eva had been created.

In 1944 it was announced that Eva had been cast as Chila Ruca in the musical film *La cabalgata del circo* (Circus Cavalcade), to be produced by the San Miguel Studios. The film became infamous for a purported feud during production between Eva and leading lady Libertad Lemarque. Lemarque would later blame the origins of the story on Eva's poor work ethic and how cast members were annoyed by the preferential treatment she received as Juan Perón's girlfriend. The film would be the last to be publicly released during Eva's lifetime. With Perón being appointed vice president and secretary of war in July, the couple began to feel much more confident in their relationship and they participated together in a Christmas programme to distribute free pan dulce (sweet bread) and cider to the population.[8]

The year 1945 would be one of the most eventful of Eva's life. She had worked her way up to become one of the highest-paid radio actresses in the country, was living with the vice president of Argentina, and was about to star in her first leading role in what would be her final film. The role of Julia in the period film *La Pródigal* strangely mirrored Eva's future as her immoral character decides one day to use her fortune for good, earning her the nickname 'the Prodigal' from her appreciative neighbours. After filming in Córdoba and at the San Miguel studios was complete, and perhaps realising that this may be her final film, Eva kept a memento in the form of a white, ruched chiffon dress with embroidered neck and cuffs that had been designed for her role in the film.[9]

Ten years on from her arrival in Buenos Aires, Eva had achieved the stardom she dreamt of as a girl in Junín. In an interview with the magazine *Radiolandia*, she reflected on her path to success:

> I am not an adventuress, although some (those who never forgive a young woman for succeeding) make me out to be one. I have spent more than five years dedicated to what is in me a firmly-rooted vocation: the arts. These have been five years of troubles, of noble struggles when I've known the uncertainty of adversity as well as the gratification of success.[10]

Notably absent from her interviews was any mention of Colonel Perón, but their relationship was exposed by the American media. A carefully inaccurate article in *Time* magazine (which would eventually be banned from sale in Argentina) described how:

> The breathless eight-month rise of Eva Duarte from artistic obscurity to one of Argentina's highest-paid radio contracts is the talk of Buenos Aries. Eva is lovely to look at – tall, svelte, brunette, alabaster-skinned, twenty-six. She is also the favourite of Colonel Juan Perón, Minister of War, and strong-boy of Argentina.[11]

Perón's support of the working class, and his relationship with Eva, became increasingly irritating to the military government. As Minister of Labour, Perón introduced a range of welfare benefits for workers: including passing a law to set minimum wages, establishing paid holidays, and ordering employers to provide severance pay. Using his authority, he was also able to assist labour unions to settle industrial disputes in exchange for their political backing. An address he delivered on 18 September, where he declared 'we've passed social reforms to make the Argentine people proud to live where they live, once again', would be the final straw for his opponents who now feared that Perón's popularity and his support from the *descamisados* might challenge the presidency of General Farrell. The US embassy, who was keeping a close eye on their South American neighbour, sent a memo on 6 September observing that Colonel Perón's star was beginning to wane due to the 'Eva Duarte connection'.

On 9 October, Perón was forced to resign from the government. Four days later President Farrell ordered his arrest, and he was taken to Martin Garcia Island. Eva quickly discovered that without Perón's position of power she was ultimately disenfranchised. Radio Belgrano's Jamie Yankelevich, a critic of Juan Perón, wasted no time in dismissing Eva from the radio station.[12] Eva would claim that 'I never felt – I say this truthfully – so small, so insignificant in my whole life like in those eight memorable days'[13] as she went door to door trying to drum up support for Perón. The extent of Eva's role in the demonstrations that followed Perón's arrest has been hotly contended. Some witnesses have her at the heart of the movement, leading demonstrators to the Plaza de Mayo. Others believe she kept in the background, while some argue that she played no part at all in organising the rally that freed Perón. It must not be forgotten that at this time, Eva was still a minor actress. She had no political influence and had lost her only means of communicating with the people upon losing her radio role. In reality, the massive rally that was held on 17 October 1945 was organised Perón's fellow military officer, Domingo Mercante, and by the various unions who supported Perón and feared losing the welfare benefits gained under his leadership. From dawn that morning, a crowd of mobilised workers, estimated between 250,000 and 350,000, gathered in the Plaza de Mayo in front of the Casa Rosada demanding Juan Perón's release. Fearful at the size of the demonstrations, the government conceded to the crowd's wish, and at 11.10pm Perón appeared on the balcony of the Casa Rosada to thank those present. The mobilisation on Loyalty Day forced Perón back into politics and his candidacy for president was announced on the Labour Party ticket the next day.

During his imprisonment, a tired Perón had written to Eva: 'Today I have written to Farrell, asking him to accelerate my retirement: as soon as I get out of here we'll get married and we'll go someplace where we can live in peace.' His commitment to make an honest woman of Eva came as a shock to the military and bourgeoisie. Why would a man who had his sights set on the presidency choose to marry an illegitimate actress with an ambiguous reputation? The truth was that Perón was in love with Eva and the couple complemented each other. Her loyalty to him during his arrest had impressed him and made him realise there was no other woman he wanted by his side. Their private civil marriage ceremony took place on the afternoon of 22 October 1945 at the Civil Registry in Junín. Family and friends met at Eva's childhood home on Arias Street, to witness Eva, dressed in an elegant ivory suit, say her vows to become Senora María Eva Duarte de Perón. Eva had finally gained the respectability she had been fighting for her entire life, but it had taken some deceit to reach that moment. As the illegitimate child of adulterous parents, Eva could never be accepted as First Lady of Argentina, and the couple realised that there would need to be some 'cleaning-up' of their origins. On the wedding certificate, María Eva Duarte stated that not only was she born in 1922, but that she was the legitimate daughter of Juan Duarte and Juana Ibarguren. After Perón was overthrown in 1955, a commission was set up to investigate the facts around Eva's birth. It discovered that at the time of her wedding, her original 1919 birth certificate disappeared and a new one was forged in Junín's civil registry that allowed Eva to finally remove any hint of illegitimacy from her life (and to knock a few years off her true age). Their religious ceremony was held in La Plata on 10 December and was followed by a short honeymoon in San Nicolás, where the couple finally got the chance to relax after a hectic few months. A tired but smiling Eva was photographed on a yachting trip alongside her new husband, looking every inch the off-duty movie star in a patterned shirt, a headscarf tied over her elaborate pompadour hairstyle, and trousers. Eva was one of the first fashionable Argentine women to appear in public wearing trousers. It is interesting that even though she conveyed her role in life to be Perón's modest and meek wife, she would choose to outwardly wear a garment that symbolically challenged traditional gender norms in a machismo society.

Upon her marriage and entry into the world of politics, a number of transformations took place to shape the new Eva Perón into the perfect political candidate's wife. First, with her job at Radio Belgrano reinstated, Eva chose to abandon her burgeoning film career to support Perón's candidacy. Her final film, *La Prodiga*, had been due for release towards the end of the year but was now deemed inappropriate due to her new political position. Perón used his influence to postpone the release, and the film wouldn't be seen by Argentines until 1984. Publicity stills and photo negatives from Eva's time as a starlet were confiscated, and evidence of her film career vanished from the archives of the studios she had worked for. Eva did not want to be haunted by her past and the removal of all traces of her acting career allowed her to construct the new image she needed to support her husband. Second, she changed her style. Eva had confessed a weakness and extravagance for clothes in interviews and was aware of the messages she could communicate through her dress. The garish colours and revealing silhouettes of her life as an actress were replaced with the beginnings of an aesthetic uniform that she would adopt in various guises until her death. Taking inspiration from Perón's military uniform and the wartime fashions of the 1940s, she started to incorporate more suits into her wardrobe, which she combined with feminine details such as peplums, prints and lace.

From 17 October 1945 to the presidential elections on 24 February 1946, Eva absorbed herself in the machinations of campaigning. She was conspicuous for being the first candidate's wife in Argentine history to accompany her husband on his electioneering tour of the country. In defiance of his advisors, Perón's admiration for Eva made him aware of how beneficial she could be to the campaign. Confident in public speaking, known to provincial audiences as an actress, elegantly dressed, and sharing the same working-class background as many of his supporters, Eva was a living example of the positive changes that Juan Perón and Peronism could bring to Argentina. It was an image that captivated the crowds and the couple capitalised on this for the next six years, nurturing the mass following that would give Perón a longer grasp on power than most of the former military leaders. Travelling on the campaign steam train, christened *El Descamisado* (the shirtless), the Peróns made a glamorous couple. To the hard-working servants and sharecropper's wives in the small villages and towns, Eva appeared like a magical Cinderella out of a fairy tale. Blonde, youthful, and dressed in her finest clothes, she stood proudly by her handsome husband's side at his speeches, but was also game to get stuck into canvassing by handing out leaflets and sermonising to the people on her love for Perón. The crowds began to call out for 'Evita', a woman they recognised as one of them who was promising the same fortune that had chanced upon her if they voted for Perón. The adoration from the people was overwhelming, and Paco Jamandreu recounted a funny anecdote of how, one morning, Eva knocked on the cabin doors of the train in her nightdress and asked the sleepy secretaries and assistants: 'Am I or am I not a goddess?' before returning to bed.[14]

Eva used the public forum that her weekly radio show granted to campaign for Perón by delivering powerful speeches urging the poor to align themselves with the Peronist movement. Her popularity and the campaign trail had highlighted the strong influence she had on the lower classes and many people viewed her as an unofficial politician. Eva also played a part in the transformation of Perón. She taught him the language of the workers and encouraged him to dress more casually to court the working classes who turned out in huge numbers to greet them and raise grievances. It is also believed that she used her knowledge of fashion to design the white military dress uniform that helped Perón to stand out from the khaki-clad crowd.[15]

The emergence of Peronism in Argentina highlighted the symbolic function that external appearances had on politics. The loyal *descamisados* embraced the term – originally applied to them negatively – as a symbol of their unionised, working-class status and their support for Peronism. The white shirts functioned as symbol of their political beliefs, distinguishing them from the other workers' subgroups, such as the communists and anarchists. Despite their hostile views, both Peronists and non-Peronists were framed by their sociological perceptions, illustrated by a particular manner of dressing and the reactions that this provoked. One of the main instigators would be Eva Perón.

Chapter 4

First Lady
4 June 1946 – 6 June 1947

24 February 1946 is a date that stands out in Argentine national history as the day that General Juan Domingo Perón was elected president, with his wife at his side. At only 26, Eva was now the First Lady of Argentina. Her position alongside her husband may have seemed challenging in such a patriarchal society, but it wasn't viewed as such because the power of a First Lady was merely an extension of her husband's. Although many upper-class Argentines derided her, Eva was living proof of the 'Argentine Dream'. Her upward mobility to First Lady was the result of her achievements and was celebrated as such by the American media in particular. Her former career as an actress also became wrapped up in the American view of actors as celebrities – no longer morally dubious characters. She was the epitome of the modern woman, and she knew she had an important part to play in justifying the participation of women in the public sphere.

Her first big challenge was to adopt an image that was respectful of her new position and her husband's office as head of state. The role of First Lady has traditionally been one of silent partner, who acts as an informal advisor or confidante to their husband. Fashion journalist Robb Young has written that a First Lady 'knows that her image will be traded as political currency and that, for the duration of her husband's tenure, she is in effect an extension of his government'.[1] Eva was never shy about her love of fashion, but she was also able to wield it as an armour against her opponents by proving that she could be a political spouse, and still look chic. The style-conscious Eva, who for the most part favoured floral dresses and extravagant hats, now had to follow the unspoken rule for political spouses by dressing to complement, and enhance, her husband's image on the domestic and world stage. It is interesting, but not surprising due to her background, that Eva chose to limit her refinements to the visual sphere that she understood, and elected not to improve her diction or deportment.

In 1946 Eva was still heavily influenced by the fashions coming out of Hollywood. Ginger Rogers would later recall a meeting with Juan Perón after Eva's death, where the president informed her that 'My wife saw every movie you made and showed them in the palace projection room. She would call in her dressmakers to copy dresses you wore. I remember the hairdresser had great difficulty trying to duplicate the various hairstyles you used with each gown.'[2] When actress Lana Turner visited Argentina in February 1946, her jewellery was seized by customs, and she later discovered that Eva had ordered each piece be photographed to be copied.

The importance surrounding what a First Lady wears is not a new phenomenon. Newspapers in America had been describing First Ladies' clothing choices since 1828.[3] Eva understood that the press and public would judge her appearance in order to define who she really was, and she used the training that she had undertaken to construct her image as an actress to put together a new visual discourse that would emulate the couture looks worn by the upper class. In the lead up to Perón's inauguration, Betty Dodero, the American-born wife of shipping magnate and Perón supporter Alberto Dodero, offered the use of her wardrobe to Eva; instead, Eva chose to earn recognition by choosing to wear 'national' brands. Eva turned to the Argentine fashion industry in her desire to surpass the elite in elegance and to symbolise the ideal Argentine woman. By wearing clothing typically reserved for the privileged, Eva was, in her own way, creating a costume for the biggest role of her life. Her use of haute couture was criticised by the upper class who viewed her as an upstart trying to conceal her true identity, while also betraying her own class. Despite Argentina's distance from the European capitals of fashion, Argentines were able to keep up to date with the latest styles being created by the top fashion houses, and by the 1920s Buenos Aires was also home to a number of established fashion houses, including Henriette, Fortuny, and a branch of the French designer Jeanne Paquin. The most prestigious fashion houses, in addition to producing their own collections, also purchased patterns and licenses to reproduce (with permission) designs by the top European couturiers, such as Balenciaga, Pierre Balmain, Marcel Rochas and Madame Grès, for their clientele.

From the day of the election until Perón was sworn in as president, Eva began to visit the boutiques of the main fashion houses in Buenos Aires. She was often accompanied by Lilian Lagomarsino de Guardo, the heiress wife of Perón's political acquaintance Dr Ricardo Guardo, and Betty Dodero. Eva was taken to the three most renowned Argentine haute couture houses: Bernarda, Henriette[4] and Paula Naletoff.[5] Even as the wife of the new president, Eva was not always instantly recognised on these shopping trips, which led to some awkward situations. When she visited Paula Naletoff's boutique one morning the designer turned Eva away saying that she had no time to attend to her. As they turned to leave, one of Eva's companions turned to Naletoff: 'Do you know who you are saying goodbye to? To the wife of the president-elect.'[6] Naletoff quickly made a phone call to issue a grovelling apology.[7]

The magnitude of Eva's new position manifested itself in a lack of confidence that was rare for her. She was unsure of the protocols that surrounded the role of First Lady and was afraid of embarrassing her husband. Her insecurity led her to ask Ricardo Guardo to recommend a designer to make suitable garments for the inauguration and accompanying events. Guardo contacted Bernarda Noci de Meneses,[8] one of his dental patients and the founder of the fashion house Bernarda, to organise an appointment. The distinguished couturier's clientele mainly comprised the anti-Peronist elite, and she cleared her schedule to avoid any hostile interactions with the wife of the new president. Guardo, completely out of his depth in the world of women's high fashion, accompanied Eva to scrutinise her choices. He later recalled that Eva was very nervous during the fitting and couldn't decide what she wanted. Guardo ultimately gained Eva's trust by advising her not to choose a violet and gold evening gown for the official inauguration banquet as the gold adornments would look inappropriate at an event where gold braid would be worn as part of the military officers' dress uniform. Eva agreed, and instead selected a silver silk evening gown (that she would come to regret for a different reason), and a black suit. Guardo was never again called upon to assist in matters of fashion.

Eva's motivation to out-dress the rich ladies who looked down their noses at her soon created a serious problem for the couture houses in Buenos Aires who agreed to dress her. Juana Palmou, an employee at Paula Naletoff, stated that 'Paula Naletoff did not want to say that she dressed Mrs Perón because the ladies of society would be reluctant to come.'[9] In order to not lose their select clientele, the couture houses began to develop two collections each season: one specially for Eva, and one for their established customers. Two of the fashion houses even sent members of staff to work with Eva as fashion assistants. Paula Naletoff sent Juana Palmou, who would later recall that her main job was:

> to have her clothes in order and to advise her on each outfit for every hour and occasion, but this was difficult because, even though Mrs Perón was modest and listened to us, she did exactly whatever she wanted afterwards (…) Because of her great personality, she didn't care about what others thought about her.[10]

The house of Henriette provided the services of their fitting room and general manager, María Asunción 'Asunta' Fernández, who would stay with the First Lady until her death and can be credited with playing a large part in the transformation of Eva's style between 1946–52. Knowing that she would be judged more closely than her husband on what she wore, Eva chose to adopt the floral dresses and tailored suits, recognisable by the shoulder pads and pencil skirts, that were popular in the mid-late 1940s. She accessorised her feminine style with peep-toe shoes and hats from Casa Giulia and Rosé Descat which crowned the elaborate pompadour hairstyles of the period that she favoured. The emergence of Peronism in the second half of the twentieth century was responsible for external appearance functioning not only as a political symbol, but also as a representation of society in Argentina.

Juan Perón was sworn in as the 35th president of Argentina on 4 June 1946. The date was specially chosen by Perón to honour the 1943 coup d'etat that had indirectly brought him to the highest office in the country, and to mark the end of Argentina's military dictatorship. Eva attended the inauguration ceremony dressed soberly in a Bernarda designed black suit with a fur-trimmed overskirt. The importance of the occasion may have played heavily on Eva's mind that day as she was photographed looking tense and gripping the arm of the vice president's wife, Maria Teresa de Quijano. Unlike the wives of other presidents, Eva was already formulating what role she would assume and how she could wield her influence. She was not willing to be a passive, decorative political consort, but she also didn't want to upstage her husband. She needed to redefine herself once again, this time into the active wife of the president.

Unfortunately, her first public misstep came on the evening of 4 June at the official banquet to celebrate the inauguration, when Eva caused a scandal by wearing the one-shoulder grey silk gown she had purchased at Bernarda. The bare shoulder would not have created such a furore if Eva hadn't had the bad luck to be seated with her bare shoulder next to Cardinal Santiago Copello. Her mistake was satirised by popular actress Sofia Bozán, who appeared on stage in a similar dress to Eva's with a sequinned cardinal bird on her bare shoulder. Photos of the event outraged 'genteel' society, who viewed the incident as another example of Eva's lack of class. Paco Jamandreu related an anecdote from July 1946, when President Perón was decorated by the Spanish government to mark the 130th anniversary of Argentine independence, which depicts Eva still finding her feet in the world of high fashion. She commissioned a green, brown and beige jersey dress from Jamandreu, but when she tried it on, she realised something was missing – jewellery. 'All the other women will come decorated like Christmas trees,' Eva declared. 'I want to surprise them by doing the exact opposite.'[11] She sent the designer out into the streets of Buenos Aires with the unenviable task of finding a simple necklace to match the dress he had designed. In a shop called La Sensación, Jamandreu struck lucky. Eva was thrilled with the bead necklace that had cost Jamandreu mere pesos and wore it proudly to the Spanish Embassy the following evening. While watching the ceremony, Eva nervously began to chew on the beads of her necklace, only to be alerted that something was wrong by her husband's laughter. The paint from the cheap necklace had stained her tongue green! If Eva hadn't already developed a tough skin in her youth, she would have done so very quickly to deflect the whispers and giggling of the upper class and the military who mocked her flamboyant appearance, dubious background and intelligence.

The new presidential couple moved into the Unzué Palace; a nineteenth-century French-style residence set in its own gardens. The property was situated out of the bustle of the centre of Buenos Aires and offered Perón easy access to his official office in the Casa Rosada. Having a large dressing room of her own was a dream come true for Eva, and she began to fill it with her collection of size 6 shoes which eventually totalled around 200 pairs. She favoured platform sandals, heels and peep-toe shoes for work and more formal events, and moccasins for private. She ordered leather sandals, heels and suede shoes from one of her favourite designers, André Perugia,[12] who was the Christian Louboutin of the 1940s.

After Perón became president, Eva was installed in an office on the fourth floor of the Central Post and Telecommunications building. Unlike former First Ladies, Eva took an active role and, even without any official position, she began to attend to the crowds of workers who were waiting for an audience with the president. On Mondays, Wednesdays and Fridays, Eva could be found intervening in labour disputes or negotiating with employers to obtain better wages for workers. This work bolstered her relationship with the Argentine trade unions and provided her with a strong power base to support the government's policies. She continued to use her radio appearances to speak directly to the *descamisados* about Perón's support for worker's rights in a natural way that the president found difficult. Eva also used her position to receive the poor and destitute to help in any way that she could. Her background gave her an empathy for the needy that former First Ladies could not relate to. By paying attention to a sector of the Argentine public who had traditionally been overlooked, Eva created a foundation for the social work that would become her life's mission. 'And we began,' she wrote in *La Razón de mi vida*. 'Bit by bit. I could not say on exactly what day. What I do know is that at first I attended to everything myself. Then I had to ask for help. And finally I had to organise the work which in a few weeks had become extraordinary.'[13]

It was at the Central Post Office that Eva first met the German-born Union Secretary, Isabel Ernst,[14] the woman who would be an influence on Eva in more ways than one. A former teacher at the Yansen school in Buenos Aires, Ernst had met and begun an extramarital affair with Perón's ally (and future Governor of

Buenos Aires) Colonel Domingo Mercante. She was given a role at the post office by Mercante, before being appointed to the National Labour Secretariat in 1944. Mercante imparted his negotiating skills to Ernst, and his credibility with the unions ultimately helped Isabel to build good working relationships with the Argentine union leadership, resulting in Perón creating the position of Trade Union Secretary of the Presidency specially for her upon his ascension to head of state. Isabel Ernst introduced the First Lady to her powerful contacts in the unions and, with her knowledge of worker's lives, collaborated with Eva on her social work. Eva would eventually ask Ernst to work for her as a private secretary and she would become a constant presence behind the First Lady. Isabel Ernst was a striking woman with short blonde hair, and it would appear that she imparted some of her fashion knowledge onto Eva, who would adopt features of Isabel's image and make them her own over time. Isabel was noted for wearing tailored, often military-inspired, suits to work, which Eva took inspiration from as she began to adopt the fabled houndstooth suit as her day-to-day office wear.

One of the key items on President Perón's agenda was widening electoral participation by granting women the right to vote. He had first raised women's suffrage in Congress as the outgoing Secretary of Labour and Welfare in August 1945. From the turn of the twentieth century, multiple feminist organisations had been formed to campaign for the rights that women in other countries were being granted. One of the most active groups of the Argentine feminist movement was the increasing female working-class. These women were not afraid to fight for improved living and working conditions, and many joined all-female labour unions to put their demands to Congress. It was in this context that Perón gave Eva the important role of spokeswoman for the campaign for women's rights in his new administration. Eva began a radio and press campaign that highlighted the need to incorporate women fully into Argentine society. Through often emotional rhetoric, Eva urged all Argentine women to view Peronism as a movement that would allow women to claim their legitimate rights. She particularly reached out to women from the lower classes to whom she could personally relate. Possibly thinking of her own mother's struggles to raise a family as a single-parent, and her own youth as a jobbing actress, Eva apparently proclaimed: 'I demanded more rights for women because I know what women had to put up with'. She also attempted to convince men to support women's suffrage by downplaying their fears that political participation would make their wives and daughters overtly masculine. Eva declared that after enfranchisement, women would become 'more feminine and attractive; they would be Peronist partners to their men'.[15] Eva often expressed contradictory feminist views – advocating for the full integration of women into Argentine society, while also declaring that she only existed to support and promote her husband. While this declaration seems highly anti-feminist today, in the machismo society of 1940s Argentina Eva was only stating what the public expected her to say as a wife and First Lady. Her independence as a working woman, blended with her vocal love for her husband, were the perfect propaganda tools to persuade women (and men) that granting women the right to vote, while empowering them, would not change women's role in society.

Even though Eva herself did not hold particularly strong feminist beliefs, she did recognise the work of feminist groups that had come before her. 'I confess,' she admitted in *La Razón de mi vida,* 'I was a little afraid the day I found myself facing the possibility of starting on the "feminist" path. What could I, a humble woman of the people, do where other women, more prepared than I, had categorically failed?'[16] Eva insisted to Congress that women were more than capable of making political decisions, while simultaneously blaming the lack of previous success for women's suffrage on the educated women of the oligarchy who had traditionally campaigned for women's rights.

For a woman so focused on her image, Eva was contemptuous of the unfeminine traits that she saw in these hardened feminists, such as a lack of care in their personal appearance, that she believed had lost them support for their cause. Eva was vocal in her criticism of Argentine feminism: 'For, not led by women but by those who aspired to be men, it ceased to be womanly and was nothing: feminism had taken the step from the sublime to the ridiculous. And that is the step I always try to avoid taking!'[17] Many of the elite and middle-class feminists joined forces for the first time in their desire to counteract the Peróns' increasing popularity with women. They wanted to gain suffrage, but not via Juan and Eva. Only months into his presidency, Perón introduced a new women's suffrage bill that was sanctioned by the Argentine Senate on 21 August 1946. It would take more than a year for the bill to pass through the House of Representatives on its way to becoming law.

On 24 September, Eva began working from Perón's former office in the Secretariat of Labour and Welfare alongside Secretary José María Freire. The move provided Eva with more space to conduct her work and allowed Perón to gradually transfer to her to all those who wished to obtain an interview with him. Eva would describe the decision for the move in her autobiography:

> I went to the Secretariat of Labour and Welfare because it was easiest for me to meet the people and their problems there; because the Minister of Labour and Welfare is a working man, and 'Evita' gets on with him frankly and without bureaucratic red tape; and also because it was there I was offered the requisite means for commencing my work.[18]

It was during this period that Eva began to move further away from the conventional duties associated with the First Ladies that had preceded her; gradually, with Perón's consent, she assumed her husband's role as champion of the Argentine working-class. Her decision to be a president's wife who broke from the traditions of her predecessors was one of the ways in which she constructed the image of 'Evita':

> I might have been a President's wife like the others. It is a simple and agreeable role: a holiday job, the task of receiving honour, of decking oneself out to go through the motions prescribed by social dictates. It is all very similar to what I was able to do previously, and I think more or less successfully, in the theatre and in the cinema.[19]

Eva's working day would begin with audiences at the Unzué Palace, where she would receive those who needed urgent assistance. She would then be driven to her office at the Secretariat to commence meetings with the poor and members of the labour unions. Eva would not leave the office until she had spoken to everyone who was waiting to see her, even if this meant working well into the night. If she had to interrupt her schedule to attend to official business or visits, she would ask those waiting to stay until she returned. Eva was assisted in her work by Isabel Ernst and Lilian Lagomarsino de Guardo. Lilian Guardo had been tasked with advising Eva on etiquette and fashion to befit her position as First Lady. Meeting with the poor and needy on a daily basis only spurred Eva on to dress more ostentatiously. By promoting her own humble origins wearing glittering jewels, Eva was implying to those she met at the Secretariat that they too could have the same opportunities as Eva, if they never forgot about their roots. Eva would always tell those who dared to suggest she tone down her image that 'They want to see me beautiful. People don't want someone old and dowdy to protect them. They all have their dreams about me and I don't want to let them down.'[20] By flaunting her power and new-found success in the faces of the upper classes, the working classes believed that Eva was representing them.

In the second half of 1946, Eva undertook the creation of what would become her life's work. The impetus for the Eva Perón Foundation had been formed after Eva was publicly snubbed by the elderly upper-class ladies of the Sociedad de Beneficiencia,[21] who undertook the majority of charity work in Argentina. Upon Perón's election, it was tradition for the First Lady to be invited to become the Sociedad's president, but no invitation was forthcoming for Eva. The ladies insisted that Eva was far too young for the position, but she knew that the real reason was that they disapproved of her background. In retaliation for their rejection, Eva set to work on her own charitable foundation using government funding that had previously supported the *Sociedad* and 10,000 pesos of her own money. After witnessing the crowds of mothers with babies, the disabled and elderly queuing in the corridors of the Secretariat of Labour and Welfare to speak with her, she knew that help was needed immediately. She used a garage at the presidential residence, that became known as 'La Tienda de las Delicias',[22] as the first warehouse to store the food and clothing that she purchased, and the donations that she received for the Foundation from supporters and the unions. After Perón went to bed, Eva could be found in the garage alongside her maid, Irma Ferrari, and private secretary, Atilio Renzi, sorting and packing the donations to be distributed among those in need.

Eva's popularity with the working classes, and Perón's faith in her, led to Eva stepping yet further outside the remit of the traditional First Lady. Beginning in October, Eva's visits to factories and to deprived neighbourhoods intensified, putting her increasingly in direct contact with those she wished to help. Simultaneously, she began to undertake official trips around Argentina. On 30 November 1946 she embarked on her first solo tour through the northern province of Tucumán. Over fifteen days, Eva was enthusiastically received wherever she went, so much so that some people were injured in the crowds that flocked to greet her. It would all be good practice for the future.

By 1947, as Eva's workload increased, her days at the Secretaríat grew longer. She didn't typically leave her office until around 10 pm each evening. During the early months of the year, she was busy formulating direct social aid that would make a difference to the lives of ordinary Argentines, focusing on employment, healthcare and housing. Alongside distributing food, household items and clothing to impoverished families, Eva involved herself in multiple projects to improve the situation for her *descamisados* and their families. Eva's dedication to the poor was evident on 20 January, when she received a delegation from the slum neighbourhood of Villa Soldati. They told her of the atrocious conditions they were living in and Eva immediately visited the area to see the problems first hand before moving the families into emergency housing. She personally implemented a plan to provide the families with health care and, by 12 February, had found new homes for all.

Eva and Perón were able to escape the pressures of government by spending weekends at the San Vicente quinta (country house), which they had purchased from Colonel Mercante in 1946. Eva adored the freedoms that the countryside retreat offered and spent time on horseback or welcoming friends and family to stay. When a series of Pinelides Fusco photographs were released of the couple in San Vicente, Eva again managed to shock members of the upper classes with her casual appearance. She was shown with her hair loose around her shoulders wearing a pair of white Bernarda trousers paired with a red cotton blouse, that she purchased prêt-à-porter from City Sport, and Harrods raffia sandals.[23] Eva was not going to be dictated to when it came to her private life.

Her public life was another matter. Her status as First Lady afforded her a highly visible platform from which she could share her personal views and personal charm. Since she held no official governmental role, Eva knew that she would never be held accountable for her husband's policies, which granted her the freedom to gain the trust of the people. Eva was extremely popular in the Argentine press during the early years of Perón's presidency, and in time this interest began to spread internationally. Her public image was subjected to ever-increasing interest and scrutiny as the North American media became fascinated with this woman who was so active in Argentine politics. *Newsweek* declared her '*la presidenta*' in August 1946, and more often than not, Eva's image was unjustly the byproduct of the North American press' view of her husband as a fascist-dictator. Just as Meghan Markle was the subject of unjust media focus during her time as a working royal, the negative aspects of Eva's life made perfect press fodder for newspapers and magazines in America. As a result, this emphasis neglected to report on the respectable aspects of her role, or the fact that in Argentina she was viewed as a powerful threat to both the oligarchy and the military. Eva's public life was viewed so unfavourably by some in Argentina that a member of the government opposition even attempted – without success – to present a bill that would have limited the First Lady's participation in public activities. This is yet another example of the views of many at the time who struggled to accept a woman – and one who grew up in poverty – in a position of power.

Perón was known to use violence against his opponents, but he preferred to cut off their access to the media. Therefore, to counteract the negative press reports about themselves, the Peróns decided to take control. Former journalist and film producer Raúl Apold joined the Undersecretariat of Press and Broadcasting in 1947, before becoming Juan Perón's propaganda chief. From the Undersecretariat, Apold orchestrated an efficient propaganda structure, managed by over a thousand employees, to support the Peronist regime. Apold rigidly enforced blacklists of those who criticised Peronism and its leaders, and would often bring legal cases against newspapers who criticised the government – or have them closed altogether. He also assisted the Peróns' purchase of Argentine press outlets in order to publish their own favourable news. Towards the end of Perón's presidency, the government would own thirteen publishing houses, seventeen newspapers, ten magazines and four information agencies.[24]

Eva was involved in controlling the government's press monopoly to her own advantage. Her career as an actress had given her the best media training she could have and her former employer, Radio Belgrano, was a victim of the Peronist media takeover. It seems that Eva was finally able to get her revenge on owner Jamie Yankelevich for firing her after Perón's arrest. After the station was formally suspended from the airwaves for airing criticism of Perón's inaugural speech, Yankelevich felt that he had no other option but to sell the company to the state, giving the Peróns full control over performers and content. One of Apold's main responsibilities, and ultimately his biggest success, was in the transformation of Eva Perón into the mythical 'Evita'. He achieved this in part through the formation of The Photographic Division, an official team of photographers who exclusively documented Eva's life through photographs. The most iconic photos of Eva Perón, some of which became seared into the Argentine consciousness, were taken by official photographer Pinélides Fusco; the embrace between Eva and Perón on the Casa Rosada balcony is one such image. Supervised by Apold, these photographs of Eva were disseminated as propaganda to convey the ethos of Perón's New Argentina. Many Argentines came to believe what they read about Eva in the press, mainly due to the lack of real information available and the censure of her past. What emerged in the Argentine media was a new Eva – the saint-like 'Evita'.

The contradiction in Eva's public persona, between the glamorous First Lady and the champion of the working class, created the perfect combination of style and social conscience that the Perón propaganda used to their advantage. The star quality that she imbued through her appearance and confident personality was like nothing ever seen before on the political stage. Eva was presented to Argentina, and the world, as the romanticised ideal of the modern Argentine woman, raised up from her humble childhood in Los Toldos to take up a position of prestige on the national stage. She was able to turn the liability of her origins into her greatest asset. Photographs showing Eva draped in fur at official functions – seen as out-of-touch by many – captured the admiration of her supporters, who understood the social significance of owning such an expensive and prized item. To her supporters, she was the people's princess who was representing a living fantasy through her style and compassion. The Peronist press moulded Eva into the poster girl for the working class, highlighting the fact that the most powerful woman in the country had not forgotten her background and would vocally continue to champion the oppressed.

Although it was Juan Perón who was elected to the presidency in 1946, it his wife who is still loved and loathed in equal measure today. The young and glamorous First Lady was a breath of fresh air with new ideas and her own ways of doing things. As early as 10 February 1947, the British Embassy had reported that Eva 'has every sign of being a woman of considerable intelligence and ambition as well as beauty'.[25] As much as Eva attempted to hide elements of her past that she knew would be disagreeable to others, such as her illegitimacy, she was proud to exploit her humble origins. As Robert Neville wrote in *Life Magazine*: 'Evita did not, to put it mildly, get where she is overnight, nor by the easy expedient of marrying a presidential candidate. Her path to power has been tortuous – a route on which a less purposeful and gritty person would have early become lost.'[26]

Chapter 5

The Rainbow Tour 6 June – 23 August 1947

In 1947, a year after being elected president, Juan Perón was invited to visit Spain by Generalissimo Francisco Franco. Franco was eager to build upon the relationship that existed between Argentina and Spain as his country found itself diplomatically isolated after the end of the Second World War. Excluded from the economic recovery program created by the Marshall Plan, Spain was in desperate need of money and food. Argentina would be the only international power to provide Franco's regime with crucial economic support when the Spanish government was placed under a UN diplomatic boycott. On 30 October 1946, the Spanish-Argentine Trade Agreement was signed which granted Spain a low interest loan of 350 million pesos for the provision of 400,000 tonnes of wheat to be delivered in 1947, and another 300,000 tonnes in 1948. The agreement would also provide a large quantity of meat, helping to create a stable market for Argentina's important meat exports. In return, Spain would provide Argentina with industrial products. This support for Spain may have had its origins in Perón's agreement with Franco's nationalist policies, but is more likely to have come from the Argentine people. Since a large percentage of immigrants to Argentina in the nineteenth and early twentieth centuries were Spaniards, many Argentines still had close family ties to the Hispanic mother country and wished to show solidarity with their forebears.

Perón was anxious to accept this politicised invitation but was aware of the damage a visit to Spain might have upon his new government and the improving relations between Argentina and the

United States. Argentina had been almost ostracised internationally for its position of neutrality during the war and was keen to build upon its membership of the newly formed United Nations. While they could appreciate the commercial and diplomatic opportunities afforded by such a trip, Perón's advisors did not think it should take place. Reports of President Perón uniting with the Caudillo would not be viewed favourably in Washington. To avoid snubbing Franco, they came up with a solution. Eva would accept the invitation on behalf of the country and travel in the president's place as a 'messenger of peace'. Perón wrote to Franco to tell him: 'I send you the heart of the Argentine.'[1] To avoid any accusations of pro-Franco sympathies, Perón's advisors added an itinerary of European countries to the trip that was fundamentally a propaganda campaign branded as a 'goodwill' tour. Scheduled to last three months, the objective of the Rainbow Tour (so called, because Eva had been styled as the 'Rainbow of Argentina') was to strengthen economic ties between Argentina and Spain and to display the Peronist government's willingness to collaborate in reconstructing Europe after the devastations of the war.

Eva was honoured to be the first Argentine First Lady to be invited on an official visit by a foreign government. The tour would offer her the opportunity to travel to Europe as the ambassadress of Argentina, and to live out a fantasy of a quasi-state visit that resembled the pleasure trips taken by the oligarchy. The Rainbow Tour would be a journey of transformation for Eva. Not only would she become a worldwide celebrity, but she would also consolidate her personal image into a recognisable style that would become synonymous worldwide with the Argentine nation and the myth of Evita. Eva would ultimately return from Europe a different woman.

As Eva would be representing the new Argentine nation in the role of ambassador, she needed to dress to impress the leaders and people of the old continent. Apart from her own wishes to display her new position of power through her clothes, Eva was also aware that she would be representing the synthesis of a young and wealthy country on the tour .[2] Her love of fashion was legendary, and before she departed to Europe, an anti-Peronist staffer reported to the press that he had recorded *Senora* Perón wearing 306 different dresses during the 270 days between 4 June 1946 and 30 April 1947.[3] This love of luxury made her advisors nervous. Eva would be visiting countries that had only recently been ravaged by war, and appearing nouveau riche in glamorous designer fashions may be perceived as a faux pas. Eva refuted these claims by stating that her appearance was of the utmost importance to her *descamisados*, who felt a sense of pride in seeing their First Lady return as a successful and wealthy woman to the birthplace of their immigrant ancestors. She would be proved right, as her Rainbow Tour would not still be remembered today if she had simply dressed not to offend. Eva purchased her clothing for the tour from four of the main fashion houses in Buenos Aires: Paula Naletoff, Henriette, Bernarda and Ana de Pombo.[4] de Pombo received a visit from two policeman in April 1947, requesting her services for the Rainbow Tour. Early the next morning she had a meeting with Eva to discuss the ensemble that the First Lady wanted to attend a reception at the Royal Palace of Madrid. In just two weeks, de Pombo and her seamstresses created a blue lace gown embroidered with rhinestones, with a matching cape of ostrich feathers that delighted the exacting Eva. She bought jewellery from Huber Ricciardi, hats and headdresses from Martin Soulés, and furs by Marcel Kummer to accessorise the sixty-four complete outfits (enough for three outfit changes a day) that would accompany her across the Atlantic.

Over 150,000 people gathered at the Presidente Rivadavia airport in Morón on Friday, 6 June to bid farewell to Eva. She addressed the crowds by telling them: 'I leave for the old world with a message of peace and hope. I am going as the representative of the workers of my country, of my beloved shirtless, with whom I leave my heart.' After a final embrace with her husband, she boarded the aircraft along with the large and varied entourage that would be accompanying her to Europe. Lilian Lagomarsino de Guardo would accompany Eva as her companion during the tour. She had initially refused to leave her children for such a length of time, but after Eva had said that she would the cancel trip if Lilian did not go with her, she finally consented. Eva would also be supported on the trip by her brother Juan Duarte (who had been appointed private secretary to the president of the republic), the shipping entrepreneur Alberto Dodero, her doctor, her private hairdresser Julio Alcaraz (who she had met during her acting days), her Jesuit confessor Father Benítez (who had travelled ahead), a speechwriter, photographers from the official 'Photographic Division', her exclusive tailor Luis D'Agostino, and her fashion advisors Juanita Palmou of the Paula Naletoff house and Asunta Fernández of the Henriette house, who would have the unenviable task of taking care of the large wardrobe.

At about half-past four that afternoon, the Iberia Douglas DC-4 plane took off. The aircraft had been specially modified on the order of General Franco for its passengers' comfort during the thirty-six-hour flight, 'with Moorish style furniture and a living room of reduced dimensions, equipped with sofa bed, armchair, coffee table, mirror and toiletries, with bedspread, upholstered armchairs and matching curtains in green velvet, among other amenities'.[5] A Douglas C-47 Dakota followed minutes later carrying the rest of Eva's entourage and the forty-six suitcases and trunks that formed her luggage. For a young woman who had only ever travelled as far as Uruguay, this trip must have felt like an adventure into the unknown. But Eva was aware of the dangers of representing her country. Once the plane reached cruising speed, she got up out of her seat to speak a warning to her fellow passengers. 'The eyes of the world are on this trip,' she told them. 'There are those who expect us to make mistakes to throw themselves on us. Watch out how they behave. Do not get up to any nonsense.'

The plane made short stopovers the following day in Brazil and the Spanish Sahara before landing in Gran Canaria on 8 June. As the plane entered Spanish airspace early that morning, in what would become a regular occurrence during the trip, Eva made use of her broadcasting skills to make her first speech as the 'Messenger of Peace' via the National Radio of Spain. Her voice could be heard by the crowds already gathering to welcome her in Madrid. After the formal greetings, Eva addressed the Canary Islanders with a staunch feminist message: 'I send a hug to all the Spanish women. I bring you a message of love and peace. Long live Spain!'[6] Eva and her entourage were then escorted to Las Palmas, where Eva was able to phone her husband from the residence of the Spanish governor. On the same day as her short visit to the Canary Islands, an Argentine ship docked at the Port of Las Palmas carrying meat, cornmeal, soap and other vital necessities that would literally save the islanders from starvation. Spaniards would name these food shipments 'Evita wheat', after the woman whose appearance represented the image of the ships loaded with wheat that had arrived in their ports.

Later that afternoon, Eva's plane took off for the short flight to Madrid, escorted by forty-one Spanish fighter jets. As the plane came into land at Barajas Airport, the pilot made two low passes over the runway to allow Eva to observe the approximately 200,000 Spaniards standing on the tarmac frantically waving white handkerchiefs and hoping to catch a glimpse of the woman they would respectfully call 'Doña María Eva Duarte de Perón' during her stay in Spain. Eva stepped from the plane wearing a tailored woollen suit with a flower on her lapel and a hat perched on the back of her head that was embellished with a large grosgrain ribbon. General Francisco Franco, his wife María del Carmen Polo, and their daughter Carmen, accompanied by the entire Spanish government, stepped forward to welcome Eva as the first notable international leader to visit Spain since the end of the civil war. Upon her arrival, Eva told the crowds 'I have come not as an axis, but as a rainbow between our two countries'.[7] She would receive all the pomp of an official state visit in recognition of Argentina's support, which Franco hoped would also helpfully divert the attention of the people from ongoing food shortages. During her stay in Madrid she resided in Franco's official residence, the opulent Palacio El Pardo. That evening, whether because of homesickness, nerves, or the fact that she was so overwhelmed by her surroundings, Eva asked Lilian to sleep in her room with her. The two women would spend the whole trip sharing a room, with Eva often spending hours talking to Lilian about the day's activities.

On Monday, 9 June, her first full day in Spain, Eva received the Grand Cross of Isabella the Catholic in a ceremony at the Pardo Palace. By knighting Eva, Franco hoped to cement international relations with Argentina. Being inducted into the Order would be Eva's crowning glory. For all those in Argentina who looked down their noses at her, she was to join a highly selective group of people in being conferred the civil honour,[8] which also granted the holder a coat of arms and an official style of address enjoyed by the Spanish nobility. For one of the most important ceremonies of her life, Eva chose to wear a black and gold lamé dress with a black toque embellished with bird of paradise feathers that fell around her face. As she finished dressing, she suddenly decided to replace the cape laid out by Asunta and Juana with a sable coat. Precisely why Eva decided to wear a fur coat on one of Spain's hottest days of the year is not known. She may have felt that she could benefit from the coat's enveloping shield on such a prominent day, or that she wanted to put her own original (and extravagant) stamp on the outfit, or she may have just wanted to garner attention for the Rainbow Tour. The coat provoked disbelief and some ridicule from those watching, but also admiration from the women in Spain who took a keen interest in what she wore.

After the formal ceremony inside the Throne Room of the Royal Palace, Eva joined Franco on the balcony to acknowledge the 500,000 people crowded into the Plaza de Oriente. Proudly displaying the red-enamelled cross of Isabella the Catholic, Eva took to the microphone to praise her host before joining the *generalissimo* in waving to the crowds. *Life Magazine* would declare that Eva performed the Falange salute, but it is difficult to tell as she often waved with her arms extended. Considering the American and British views of the Rainbow Tour, they took it as a sign of Eva's fascist sympathies and would triumphantly report on Eva's missteps and humiliations during the rest of the tour. The day finished with a gala dinner followed by a ballet performance at the Palacio El Pardo, during which Eva wore her new award over the blue dress and dramatic ostrich feather cape designed by Ana de Pombo specially for the occasion.

The following morning, after addressing the Spanish people over the radio, Eva visited the National Handicrafts Market accompanied by Carmen Polo. The party then travelled to the Palace of San Lorenzo de El Escorial where, to Carmen Polo's chagrin, Eva was an hour late for the planned tour after stopping to change into a green patterned suit. As Eva toured the building, she endeared herself less to Carmen Polo by stating, 'Why don't you dedicate this enormous building to something useful? For example, a colony for poor children, you see so many!' In the early afternoon, she visited the camp of the National Delegation of the Youth Front. Throughout these visits Eva's charitable nature saw her hand out 100 peseta notes to the poor children she met along the way. Her 'Lady Bountiful' nature symbolised Argentina's wealth for many of the Spanish lower classes. It was in this context that Franco organised an evening celebrating Spanish folklore in the Plaza Mayor to honour Eva's visit. It was past midnight before the guest of honour made her entrance. Wearing a long white fur coat over a black and white evening gown, Eva was escorted to the constructed grandstand by Lilian and Carmen Franco, where she took her seat alongside the *generalissimo* and his wife. The entertainment ended with a special gift for Eva. Representatives from each of Spain's fifty provinces presented Eva with examples of their provincial costumes tailormade to her measurements. The collection composed of over 720 pieces, including underwear, shawls, shoes, headdresses and jewellery. The artisans had embroidered Eva's initials and affectionate messages, such as 'We love you Evita' into the costumes. For the daughter of a seamstress to be honoured in such a way must have been an emotional moment. Eva would consider the collection to be among her most valuable possessions, and upon her return to Argentina she asked the Museum of Decorative Art in Buenos Aires to display the garments in an exhibition. The costumes would remain in storage in the basement of the Unzué Palace,[9] where Paco Jamandreu would recall Eva being taken during the last months of her life to look at them and reminisce about the tributes that were paid to her in Spain.

After the previous tiring day of touring a number of Castilian cities, Thursday, 12 June saw a return to local activities. Eva spent the morning receiving dignitaries and important visitors before setting off with Carmen Polo to visit the Museo Nacional de Artes Decorativas on the western edge of the Retiro Park. Eva wore a hooded cape over a floral dress, while Carmen Polo competed with her Argentine guest in a blue tailored suit and a straw hat with her trademark pearl necklace. The two women had much in common. Both were First Ladies married to military men who had become the leader of their respective countries. Eva and Carmen Polo equally exerted a major influence in censoring the press in Argentina and Spain, and they were also both known for their glamorous appearances, which made much use of their large personal collections of clothes, hats and jewellery. But their similarities did not make for friendship. Franco and Carmen wanted to show off Spain's historical heritage, but Eva insisted on speaking to ordinary Spaniards and visiting working-class neighbourhoods. She believed that she had come to Spain as a woman of the people, but Carmen Polo viewed all workers in Spain as 'reds' due to their participation against her husband in the civil war. Eva spoke her mind when she reminded *Doña* Carmen that her husband didn't govern Spain as a result of votes (like Perón), but because of his victory in the civil war. Carmen tried to stay hospitable but the differing views of the two women often led to disputes over the itinerary during Eva's time in Spain.

In the afternoon, the mayor of Madrid, José Moreno Torres, invited Eva to attend a bull fight in her honour at Las Ventas. Eva arrived an hour late with her hosts, dressed in a white brocade suit accessorised with a black mantilla. She was not afraid of voicing her distaste for the bloodsport, 'I don't like it! I'm sorry, but to me it is a barbaric spectacle.'[10] Something that was more to Eva's taste was shopping. During her time in Madrid, she visited a branch of Balenciaga's Spanish outlet, Eisa, to make some purchases. As Eisa garments were made in Spain, they were usually less costly than their Parisian equivalents. Eva's sisters Erminda and Blanca would later attest that Balenciaga was one of their sister's favourite designers. The day ended with a gala dinner for Eva hosted by the Madrid City Council that was attended by 119 people, including Franco and his ministers. The party then moved to the El Teatro Español to watch a performance of Lope de Veja's *Fuenteovejuna*.

The first part of Eva's fifth day in Spain was spent in Toledo, where she visited an orphanage and met veterans of the Spanish Civil War. On her return from Toledo, she was taken to the University City Home to see some of the works undertaken by the Auxilio Social Falangist welfare organisation. Eva was introduced to Mercedes Sanz-Bachiller Izquierdo, the founder of the charity, who, given Eva's keen interest in the subject, explained how the charity operated to provide children's homes, medical care and women's education throughout the country. Eva would use what she learnt during this visit to form and inspire her Eva Perón Foundation, still in the development phase during her Rainbow Tour.

After another late night spent attending a party in the Retiro Park, Saturday was another busy day that saw the *Señoras* Perón and Polo explore the University City and the Prado Museum. Eva attended a reception given by the Argentine diplomatic mission, where she was received by the ambassador Pedro Radio, members of the diplomatic staff, and a group of Argentine expatriates now living in Madrid. In a not-so-subtle dig at Carmen Polo, Eva led a toast to Argentine and Spanish workers before returning to rest for the afternoon at the Palacio El Pardo. Shortly before 6pm in the evening, Eva and Carmen Polo were escorted by the Minister of Labour around a social housing project and the Workers' Training School, where Eva would address the workers with a speech extolling the virtues of Perón's policies and the *descamisados*.

As Eva's last day in Madrid drew to a close, she broadcast her 'Rainbow speech' from the Palacio El Pardo. Aimed at the women of Spain and Argentina, she told them:

> In this hour of rapid transition, we form part of a social revolution that reaches not only with worker and his just claim that society consider him a human being with a transcendent and immortal soul, but also the woman who demands all the rights she needs to develop her own powerful talents.[11]

While stressing the importance of family, Eva also encouraged women to aspire to be doctors and politicians. The *generalissimo* was not fond of this type of left-wing rhetoric, especially coming from a woman. Franco found Eva's involvement in politics hard to swallow. He believed that women should conform to the traditional roles of wives and mothers, and that they should play no role in public life. He must have been glad that he wouldn't be burdened with her for much longer, as she continued her tour. To thank her hosts for their warm hospitality, Eva organised a dinner at the exclusive Hotel Ritz on her final night. Only a few years previously, Eva would have been excluded from the hotel owing to its '*No tipo Ritz*' policy that refused to admit actors to the hotel. Times had changed and by appearing in a form-fitting strapless gold lamé gown adorned with Van Cleef & Arpels diamonds, her pompadour hairstyle accessorised with a matching gold lamé scarf; Eva proved that.

Following mass in the El Pardo, Eva spent most of Sunday, 15 June bidding her farewells to the city officials who had made her visit to the city such a success. Franco gifted her the priceless tapestry that would form the backdrops of her official photographs in the Unzué Palace. That evening, dressed in a lilac and white polka dot silk suit and a straw hat, she stood waving from the plane door to the crowds who had gathered. She would never see the city again in life, but her body would make its long-awaited return to Buenos Aires from Barajas Airport twenty-seven years later.

Eva's tour of the Spanish interior continued with a visit to the autonomous community of Andalusia. Arriving in Granada, Eva, who had changed her outfit on the flight, was wearing a polka dot dress and a floral headdress. During festivities held at the City Hall on Eva's first evening in the city, her brother and Albert Dodero snuck out to the adjacent neighbourhood of Sacromonte where they enjoyed an evening of drinking and flamenco with the Granadian Romani. When news of the incident made its way back to Eva, she erupted at her brother. She knew that any whiff of scandal would be picked up by the press as an example of Eva's unsuitability to be First Lady. She told Juan in no uncertain terms that one more mistake would result in him being sent home. As if nothing untoward had happened, the following morning, Monday 16 June, Eva toured the Generalife, stopping to sign autographs and shake the hands of the people who lined the streets, before making her way to Granada Cathedral. Her entrance into Seville that evening saw her feted as royalty with a horse-drawn carriage procession through the streets.

By the morning of Wednesday the 18th, Eva was exhausted. She cancelled some of the scheduled events in Seville and chose to rest in her suite at the Hotel Alfonso XIII, for the first time since her arrival in Spain ten days previously. In the afternoon she travelled to the historic city of Huelva, where she visited a flamenco festival and enjoyed a boat cruise of the city sites. She did not return to her hotel until 1.30 am the next morning. Galicia was next on the tour schedule, where Eva was awarded Santiago de Compostela's Gold Medal during a reception at the Palacio de Rajoy. From there she travelled by car to Pontevedra. The streets during the 2½ hour journey were filled with Spaniards cheering for her. The enthusiastic support shown to her during the tour of Spain was remarkable. The Spaniards had so much to be grateful to Eva and Juan Perón for, that Eva would find her reception throughout the rest of Europe a shock.

On 20 June, while Eva reviewed the troops at the Naval Military School in Marín, Juan Perón sat down with the Spanish Ambassador and his secretaries in the Unzué Palace to watch a news recording of his wife's arrival into Madrid. The rapturous reception she received was more than the government could have hoped for. Eva's photogenic qualities and charitable donations had garnered international press attention for the Spanish portion of the Rainbow Tour, on which it was reported that Franco had spent $4 million. Most of the costs incurred by Eva, such as hotel accommodation and telephone calls, were actually taken care of by the Argentine government and Alberto Dodero.

The next day Eva flew to Zaragoza. She was dressed smartly in a printed dress, black coat and black hat, befitting the importance of her visit to the Cathedral-Basilica of Our Lady of the Pillar. The archbishop invited her to pray at the shrine of Our Lady of the Pillar, a privilege usually reserved for the most important Spaniards. Eva appeared visibly moved by the honour as she kissed the mantle and the wooden statue of the Blessed Virgin Mary. She took off the pair of gold earrings that she was wearing and left them on the shoulder of the statue as an offering. This gesture, along with the large bouquet of orchids that she would have delivered to the shrine, drew attention to her public devotion to the Catholic Church. Throughout her tour of Spain, Father Benítez ensured that Eva was photographed attending mass and praying, with the ultimate goal of proving to the Vatican that she should be honoured upon her arrival in Rome. In the wake of another late night as the guest of honour at a banquet, in which she was attired in a pale blue dress and white fur stole, Eva was so tired that she copied a letter Lilian was writing to her husband almost word for word and sent it as her own to Perón.

Eva's last stop in her tour of Spain was Barcelona, where she was greeted by Carmen Polo and her daughter on the runway at El Prat airport. So many people had turned out to see her that the open-top car procession took half an hour to cover the 7½ mile journey to the Palacio Real de Pedralbes. Eva was genuinely thrilled by the rapturous welcome and stood in the car to wave at those lining the route. She spent the majority of Sunday 22 June speaking to workers' delegations from Barcelona at the Palacio. Father Benítez found her stressed, on account of a lack of sleep and strict Spanish protocol. Eva's grasp on time was never great, and she allowed these meetings to overrun, with the result that she did not begin to get dressed for a dinner at the City Hall that started at 9pm until gone 10.30pm. Her punctuality had become a major problem. Not only did it complicate life for those organising the tour schedule, but it also annoyed Carmen Polo, who was often left waiting for *Señora* Perón, and embarrassed Lillian, who had to make excuses for her. Eva's lateness had never really bothered her (mainly because she was allowed to continuously arrive late as no one was brave enough to raise her timekeeping with her). Being late may have given Eva the feeling that she had more authority over her life, which had become much more regimented upon Perón's election. When Asunta mentioned that the people who were waiting on the guest of honour might be annoyed, Eva told her not to worry. 'No one imposes a schedule on me,' she retorted. Almost three hours late, Eva and Carmen Polo finally arrived at the City Hall. The guests didn't make it to the performance of *A Midsummer's Night Dream* in the Montjuich Gardens' Teatre Grec until 3am, when Eva swept in as a fairy queen dressed in fur and diamonds. Before getting some sleep that morning, Eva took advantage of the time difference to phone her husband to tell him about her triumphant entry into the city.

Monday began with the welcome news that Pope Pius XII would receive Eva in Rome. After spending the morning resting, she took to the stage at the Palacio Nacional in Montjuic to speak to a large meeting of workers and labour leaders. Juan Perón also addressed the meeting in a radio broadcast in which he told the workers: 'I have no words to express my gratitude for the demonstrations of affection that you are showing to me wife who at this time represents a head of state and a whole people.'[12] As 23 June was the Night of San Juan (Juan Perón's Saint Day), Eva was invited to celebrate the summer solstice at Barcelona's Royal Tennis Club. With much delay, Eva and Carmen Polo arrived at 2am and left after only fifteen minutes.

Eva's visit to the home of her ancestors resonated with America, and the American press joined their European counterparts in publishing articles disseminating Eva's every move and her speeches, as well as describing her clothes. The publishing group Time Inc. followed Eva's tour closely and strove to demonstrate the fascist sympathies of the Peronist regime. The 23 June 1947 edition of *Time* featured an article with the suggestive title 'ARGENTINE: Dashing Blonde', that declared: 'Madrid belonged to Evita last week.'[13] The piece drew political comparisons between Heinrich Himmler's reception in Spain in 1940 with that of Eva. However, the article did have to point out that Eva's arrival in Madrid had drawn out even larger crowds than had ever turned out for the *generalissimo*. 'Of course,' *Time* explained, 'she's better looking.'[14]

Generalissimo Franco arrived in Barcelona on Tuesday the 24th to preside over the final banquet to honour Eva's visit. A huge stage was constructed in the centre of the Plaça de Sant Jaume in preparation for a folk festival that would follow the dinner. The Francos and Eva left the Palacio Real de Pedralbes at ten that evening and did not return before three. The final day of Eva's strenuous Spanish itinerary saw the tired First Lady suffer an emotional breakdown in her rooms within the Palacio. She felt unworthy of the tributes that the Spanish had made to her during her visit and bemoaned her illegitimate status to Father Benítez. Benítez had the opportunity to boost Eva's confidence at that moment by admitting that Juan Perón was also born out of wedlock, but he chose to remain silent and let Eva think that it was only marriage to her husband that legitimised her. Eva's thoughts remained on her background when she took to the airwaves of Radio Nacional de España in the afternoon to address the Spanish people. She told the Spanish workers:

> You have exalted yourselves, … who rightly demand that the old Society in which some beings, by virtue of having been born into opulence, enjoyed all immunities, should never be re-established; and other beings, because of the sin of being born into poverty, had to suffer all the obligations. Obscure lineage and poverty will no longer put-up barriers to anyone to achieve the development of their aspirations and the triumph of their ideals.[15]

Just before 6pm, Eva thanked her hosts for the final time on the runway at El Prat airport. She gave Carmen Polo a hug, but it was evident that there was no love lost between the two women who had shared so much together those last few weeks. The women's much publicised style battle also came to end the moment Eva boarded the DC-4 aircraft. Even though the *generalissimo* and *Doña* Carmen may have been relieved to see Eva on her way, the Argentine government considered the tour to have been a diplomatic success so far.

The reception that Eva would receive in Italy was to be very different to what she was leaving behind in Spain. Italy would not be so receptive to her charms. After the fall of Mussolini's fascist regime, and the establishment of the Italian Republic, Italians were faced with the monumental task of rebuilding their country. Argentina had once again stepped forward to offer a financial agreement to allow the Italian government to buy food. Even though the Christian Democrat government may have been wary of Perón's public praise for Mussolini, they knew they could be nothing but hospitable to the First Lady of the country who was keeping their citizens from starving. But not everyone was keen to roll out the red carpet for a woman who had just been feted as a queen without a crown by the fascists of Spain.

Eva arrived at Rome's Ciampino Airport where she was greeted by the Chancellor of Italy, Count Carlo Sforza, who accompanied her in a convoy of cars to the Argentine embassy. Thirty thousand Romans packed the streets, considerably less than in Spain. It didn't take long for Eva to meet with protests on this new stage of her tour. Outside the embassy, a large group of communists had gathered and shouted obscenities at *Señora* Perón. They were quickly arrested but Eva now knew that winning over Italy was going to prove a bigger challenge.

Eva awoke on Friday 27 June knowing that one of the most important days of the Rainbow Tour was upon her. There has never been an Argentine government so identified with the Catholic Church as the one presided over by President Perón. The alliance between Peronism and the church lay in their shared dedication to social justice, in which both agreed the state had a key part to play. Eva had rehearsed repeatedly with Father Benítez for the long-awaited visit to Pope Pius XII and believed she had publicly affirmed her devotion to the church through her speeches and support of her husband's religious policies to be awarded accordingly. Just before 10am in the morning, Eva left the Argentine Embassy (with a large police escort to prevent any further protests) on her way to the Vatican. She was dressed in a floor-length black silk crêpe dress with a flowing black veil pinned into her hair that conformed to the protocol for papal audiences. The dress was made by Olimpia Ogando at the House of Bernarda, based on a design by the French couturier Madame Grès. A small brooch was sewn into the hem of the dress that, when raised, could be fastened to give a cloak effect. Eva knew that her ensemble on such a special occasion would be meticulously studied and analysed. Therefore, she chose to wear only one piece of jewellery – the Grand Cross of Isabella the Catholic. Eva was afforded a thirty-minute interview with the Pope in the Vatican library. Even though no official transcript of their conversation has ever been released, a member of the papal household implied that Pius XII had shown his appreciation for the assistance provided by Argentina to Europe after the war. To Eva's displeasure, the Pope did not bestow an official title upon her, which would have been an honour that her critics couldn't overlook. Instead, the Pope awarded Juan Perón with the Grand Cross of the Order of Pius IX, one of the highest papal orders of knighthood, for his service to society and the church. Eva was gifted a rosary. Rumours abounded that her critics had sent a dossier to the Pope detailing her murky path to power. Knowing that she could not vent her anger at this perceived snub publicly, Eva had already instructed Alberto Dodero that if she was not granted a papal honour then her expected donation to the Vatican would be a modest one. After touring the Sistine Chapel, Eva was ordered to rest by her doctor, who had noticed the physical and emotional toll that the relentless tour schedule, and oppressive summer heat, were taking on the First Lady.

During her stay in Rome in 1947, Eva was able to indulge her passion for fashion by purchasing garments and shoes from two of the biggest Italian designers of the period; Fernanda Gattinoni[16] and Salvatore Ferragamo.[17] Gattinoni had been the director of the fashion house of Ventura throughout the war before founding her own atelier on the Via Marche in 1945. Her minimalist designs were an unusual choice for Eva at the time. The fashion journalist Irene Brin wrote in 1951: 'Fernanda … dressed Eva Perón, usually decked out in feathers and flounces, in ultra-simple Lombard silks.'[18] Eva's patronage of shoe designer Salvatore Ferragamo would last until her death and would entwine the names of the First Lady and the designer forever. Ferragamo remembered Eva as a demanding client:

> I remember the fantastic requests of Eva Perón, one of the most intelligent women I have ever met. She had the wildness of the Andes in her feet and the wildness of extravagance in her demands. There are some skins which are uncommercial because they are too rare, or too heavy, or cannot be processed, or are too small. Eva Perón dismissed all difficulties. She must have the skins she demanded, not only the fairly common llama, but armadillo, lizard, and every rare reptile. Some of the shoes had to be painted with oils because the skins would not take dye, and others had to be dusted with gold and silver. They were the most extraordinary shoes I have ever made, and the prices I was forced to charge were astronomical.[19]

The designer would declare that the size of a woman's foot was key to her character and divided his clients into three categories: the Venus, the Aristocrat and the Cinderella. Ferragamo observed that the Cinderella client, who took a shoe smaller than a size 6, is essentially 'a feminine person, a lover of jewels and furs, who must be in love to be truly happy'.[20] Naturally, Eva took a size 5B.

Eva's arrival in Milan on Sunday 29 June coincided with a shake-up to her schedule in Italy. Officially, she should have travelled onwards from Milan to Venice, where everything was ready for her visit, before touring other cities in the north of the country. The public reason given for the cancellations blamed the high temperatures, but the truth was that the Italian government were becoming worried about ensuring *Señora* Perón's safety. Alberto Dodero came to the rescue by offering Eva the use of his villa on the Italian Riviera to recuperate during her unexpected free time. Before leaving to attend a performance at La Scala on the evening of 2 July, Eva requested an audience with the chancellor, Count Carlo Sforza. In a gesture of forgiveness, she requested that the thirty communist protestors who were arrested outside the Argentine embassy in Rome be released. Whether she hoped this might convince the communists to not disrupt her tour any further, or was a genuine gesture of goodwill, the Count agreed to take care of the matter. Sforza and Eva arrived at the opera just in time to catch the beginning of the third act.

Eva arrived back in Rome on Monday 7 July, where she spent her time visiting the sites, including the Forum, the Colosseum and the Borghese Gallery. Her next stop on the Rainbow Tour was to be in England. Negotiations between Buenos Aires and London had begun in May after it was announced by the Argentine press that Eva had been invited by His Majesty's Government to visit the United Kingdom. As no official invitation had actually been issued, the British government felt pressurised to graciously extend an offer to host Eva so as not to offend an important economic trade partner who provided Britain with much-needed food supplies.[21] As the United Kingdom was still under austerity measures after the war, the country had not hosted a state visit since 1939. The government therefore took the line promoted by the Argentine Minister of Foreign Affairs, Atilio Bramuglia, that the Rainbow Tour was undertaken privately and unofficially by Eva. The Argentine

Ambassador was thus informed that Eva would be welcomed as a distinguished foreign guest in Britain on her planned dates at the end of June. Pierson Dixon, the Principle Private Secretary to the Foreign Office, wrote to King George VI's Private Secretary, Sir Alan Lascelles, to communicate that 'This, in fact, is not an official invitation to come here, but in view of the forceful character of the lady and her evident determination to be received in a grand manner in England, it will certainly be interpreted as such by her.'[22]

The government's fear that Eva's visit to Britain, coming so soon after her publicised visit to General Franco, would be misconstrued by the British public quickly became a reality. While some tabloids announced that Eva's visit would culminate in a much-needed cash-boost for the government through the purchase of warplanes for the Argentine military, others openly stated that 'The president's wife is not welcome'.[23] As public opinion started to turn on the upcoming visit, members of Parliament began to debate the suitability of welcoming the woman many viewed as the wife of a fascist dictator into the country. One Labour lawmaker tried to defend Eva by comparing her to American First Lady Eleanor Roosevelt, while a Conservative MP asked why the red carpet should be rolled out for a woman who had recently been celebrated by Franco. It would be Eva herself who would decide the fate of the trip when the planned dates for her visit were suddenly changed by the Argentine delegation to the 15–19 July. These dates coincided with the royal family's summer residence at Balmoral and the Argentine Ambassador in London was tasked with travelling to Italy to meet with *Señora* Perón to tell her that it would now not be possible to meet with Queen Elizabeth. Eva was extremely unhappy that her hopes of being admitted into Buckingham Palace and sitting down for tea with actual royalty were dashed. The Duchess of Gloucester graciously indicated that she would meet with Eva, but the First Lady was not used to being snubbed on her tour. The British government prepared themselves to issue a statement if Eva or her entourage decided to publicly blame the unwillingness of the Queen for the cancellation of the visit.

As late as 9 July, the Argentines and the British attempted to rearrange the visit to 25 July to allow Eva to attend a garden-party at Buckingham Palace on that date with the King and Queen, but Eva was still insisting that she would not grace the country with her presence unless the visit was regarded as official. She believed that every country she had visited so far had offered her that courtesy, yet an official telegram sent to the Foreign Office from the British Ambassador to Italy, Sir Noel Charles, told a different story. Charles stated that when he had questioned the Italian Prime Minister and Minister for Foreign Affairs about whether their invitation to Eva had been official, 'They were rather amused and admitted they had been bounced into doing more than had originally been intended. The invitation was originally semi-official … and the lady had contrived to obtain more and more by the simplicity of her approach.'[24] President Perón pragmatically urged his wife to accept the British itinerary with its planned visits to the BBC, Wimbledon, and a fashion show, as better than nothing, but he hadn't bargained on his wife's wounded pride. She called the Argentine Ambassador in London and told him to cancel her visit. If the British wouldn't bend to her wishes, then they would forego the chance to welcome the 'Rainbow of Argentina' to their shores.

During Eva's visit to Italy, *Time Magazine* published a cover story in their 14 July edition captioned 'Eva Perón: Between two worlds, an Argentine rainbow'. The cover portrait of Eva, created by Boris Chaliapin, marked the first time that a South American First Lady appeared alone on the cover in the periodical's history.[25] She was also only the third woman to appear on the cover by 1947, having been preceded by actress Deborah Kerr and Princess Elizabeth. The Rainbow Tour had transformed Eva into a truly international personality whose image was being projected around the globe. The lengthy article, titled *Little Eva*, attempted to summarise

Eva's trip up to that point. It described 'the triumphal tour of Argentina's beryllium-bright First Lady'[26] as being the talk of the town in Buenos Aires. A central theme, as in most press reports throughout her life – and after her death – was her clothes. The article considered that her use of jewellery and numerous clothing changes for her appearances made her an unbeatable force. Eva's perceived lack of class was something that the press particularly liked to highlight. The article repeated the story where an Italian reporter asked Eva if she had a favourite author. 'Why do people ask me questions like that? I like everything I read,' she replied. When pressed, she answered, 'Plutarch. He's an ancient writer.'[27] Eva's lack of culture was blamed on an upbringing that was unique among First Ladies, and the press liked to accentuate the belief that 'good taste' was inherited and could not be acquired with money or via the political power of her husband. This trip would ultimately prove these assumptions wrong. As it was the first to mention Eva's illegitimate status, the article did not find favour in Argentina, which resulted in *Time* being banned from sale in the country for several months.

With the visit to Britain cancelled, and nothing scheduled until the trip to France, Eva and her entourage enjoyed ten days of rest and relaxation on the Italian Riviera. For the first time on the whole trip, Eva was able to experience life as a tourist. She woke late, took long walks along the beach, went shopping with Lilian, and spoke to her husband for hours on the telephone. It was in Italy that one of the most recognisable features of Eva's appearance began to take shape – her iconic chignon. Julio Alacaraz's elaborate hairstyles had caused numerous delays during the trip and did not always flatter Eva. Lillian also knew that Perón wasn't a fan of his wife's flamboyant elaborate hairstyles either and she approached Alcaraz to suggest styling Eva's hair into a chignon. It is not surprising that Eva agreed to this chic style as she had long admired the Polish artist Tamara de Lempicka, and it is very possible that Tamara influenced Eva's new style transformation. In Rapallo, the evolution of her style as First Lady came to the fore when she was photographed wearing a tabard-style top with a wolf, the emblem of Rome, embroidered on the pocket. By paying homage to her host country through her dress, Eva was showing that she understood the diplomatic power of fashion. Father Benítez was the only member of Eva's entourage who was concerned about how images of this holiday on the Riviera may be construed when Eva should have been on a working tour. He knew that the date for the upcoming French visit was set with no possibility of being altered. Therefore, he contacted the Argentine government and asked if there was the possibility of organising a short trip to Portugal to end what he viewed as *Señora* Perón's enforced idleness. Portugal's dictator, António de Oliveira Salazar, was honoured by the request and promptly offered a formal invitation to Eva.

The four days Eva spent in Portugal, between 17 and 20 July, passed in a blur of workers' meetings and visits to social projects undertaken by the Salazarist government. Eva espoused the benefits of Peronism to everyone she met, including the exiled Umberto II of Italy. She caused consternation to her advisors when she had an interview with Infante Juan, Count of Barcelona, heir to the defunct Spanish throne. Worries about how *Generlissimo* Franco may interpret the meeting were waved away by Eva who defined herself as a 'messenger of peace'. As Eva boarded the plane to depart Portugal for Paris, Alberto Dodero and Juan Duarte gave a brief statement to the press informing them that the tour's schedule had been rearranged again to now include a holiday in Cannes, Monte Carlo and Biarritz. The fatigue of the tour was not only reinventing the planned itinerary, but Eva herself.

After the austerity of Portugal, Eva was looking forward to a return to the pomp and ceremony that the French visit would involve. She disembarked from the plane at Orly Airport on Monday 21 July dressed head to toe in white, with a large ruby brooch offering the only pop of colour to her ensemble. She had saved her finest clothes for Paris, where she knew they would be appreciated by the French arbiters of fashion. In the forty days since she had arrived in Europe, the stylish *señora* who arrived in Paris was a vast improvement from the gaudy woman who had worn a fur coat in Spain. Whereas she knew her reception in Madrid would be triumphant, she was unsure about the French and perhaps felt that they would appreciate her new chic look. She was met on behalf of the French government by the Foreign Minister and former French Resistance fighter, Georges Bidault, who escorted her in a convoy of forty cars to the Ritz Hotel. The Suite Impériale, usually the reserve of royalty, was put at Eva's disposal for her stay.

The same night as her arrival into the 'City of Lights', she attended a reception at the Maison de l'Amerique Latine on Boulevard Saint-Germain. Eva wore one of her most show-stopping outfits for the occasion – a strapless, fitted gold lamé gown with a long gold veil in her hair that fell to the floor. Accessorised with diamond jewellery and studded gold heels that caught the light as she lifted her train to descend the marble staircase on the arm of Argentinean Ambassador Julio Roca, it was not surprising 'that the Latin American diplomats who were presented to her behaved as she were royalty, the ladies retreating three steps and curtsying'.[28] The Cleopatra-like image she presented that night harked back to her days as an actress and an obsession with veils, from which Paco Jamandreu had tried to dissuade her. To dress so elaborately was to court attention and exert her political power. The evening's host, Jacques Soustelle, organised a small press conference towards the end of the festivities. Eva's authentic honesty to the journalists' questions was rare for a political spouse. She acknowledged that her views on the Catholic Church had been formed by her childhood experiences: 'I do believe in the church although it is unpleasant to find it more political than spiritual … The priest did not want to give me First Communion because I did not have a white dress like my companions.' Eva's health was put under spotlight when she was asked if she was pregnant. She replied: 'They asked me the same thing in Spain. Argentines never ask such questions. As far as I know, Madame Stork has not set me a card announcing her visit.'[29] Before retiring to bed at 1am in the morning, Eva made sure to phone her husband. They discussed the press photographs taken of her that Perón forwarded from Buenos Aires and the upcoming schedule. The tour was the longest time the couple had been apart since they had first met, and both agreed that Eva was beginning to visibly languish. The Duke de Brissac, who had earlier that evening kissed Eva's hand, later told his friends: 'She is very beautiful, yet she carried death on her face. I don't give her even five more years to live.'[30] His prophecy would be remarkably accurate.

Unlike her time in Spain, Eva made sure to attend all her appointments in Paris on time. Her second day began with a luncheon hosted by President Auriol and his wife Michelle at the Château de Rambouillet. Eva had long been fascinated by Marie Antoinette since she saw Norma Shearer's portrayal of the doomed queen and was excited to look around the famed Laiterie de la Reine. This visit prompted protests from the French Communist Party who were angry at the royal treatment she was being given, but passed without incident and Eva was mainly unaware of the resistance to her visit. She continued her tour of the city with trips to the main tourist sites, including Napoleon Bonaparte's tomb, the Chamber of Deputies, the Eiffel Tower and Notre Dame.

The tour suffered a setback on Wednesday morning when Eva fainted from exhaustion. Her doctor had been worried about her fragile health for some time and ordered that the day's planned activities be cancelled or rearranged. Eva had been looking forward to attending an exclusive fashion show arranged by Marcel Rochas but cancelled when her entourage advised her against it for fears of presenting a frivolous image. Knowing how much Eva loved fashion, Alberto Dodero came to the rescue again. Later that afternoon, Christian Dior,[31] Jacques Fath[32] and Marcel Rochas sent members of their staff with trunks of couture to Eva's suite at The Ritz. Eva's usurpation of the Argentine oligarchy crossed a new line with the Parisian couture houses choosing to come to her. Unlike the rest of Europe, the wealth in Argentina made Eva a promising client for the three designers who were starting out in their successful careers. It would be Christian Dior who would save Eva from appearing as a dated Hollywood starlet by offering her the elegant and feminine styles that would unlock the final chapter in her Cinderella transformation. From their first meeting during the Paris trip, Eva 'ordered several outfits from Dior, from suits to coats, gowns and dresses – all the day and evening wear required to dress a women who had grown up marvelling at Hollywood and who ruled her country like a sovereign.'[33]

Eva's visit to France was scheduled to coincide with the signing of a trade agreement between France and Argentina that would, by means of a loan, see Argentina supply the French with much-needed wheat and meat. In a solemn ceremony held in the Ministry of Foreign Affairs on the Quai d'Orsay, Eva watched as Argentine Ambassador Julio Roca, and French Foreign Minister George Bidault signed on behalf of their respective governments. Eva's choice of a metallic dress and lavish Van Cleef & Arpels jewellery for the occasion became a matter of state when 'One French commentator quipped unkindly: "Madame Perón will be made palatable to the French workers and peasants by being dressed as a piece of Argentine frozen beef."'[34] This direct criticism of Eva's extravagance while the French were still struggling with food rationing would be something that would be repeated as she transformed herself into Evita. After the signing ceremony concluded, the French government expressed its appreciation to Argentina by awarding Eva with the Legion of Honor. An awkward moment followed as George Bidault was tasked with pinning the honour to Eva's strapless gown. After looking to his colleagues for help, he managed to find a few folds of fabric around the neckline to pin the cross to without any impropriety. For Eva, the order of merit was a symbol of how far she had come and truly ascertained her status as First Lady of Argentina.

The itinerary for Thursday 24 July would be a stark reminder for Eva of the destruction that the Second World War had wreaked on France. She spent the morning with *Madame* Bidualt and Lilian speaking with members of the National Federation of Deported and Imprisoned Resistance Fighters and Patriots. Eva was largely unaware of the atrocious crimes committed by the Nazis during the war and was shocked to see and hear about the sufferings of prisoners in concentration camps. Before departing, she left a large donation for survivors of the Holocaust. She was then escorted around the Maison d'enfant de Sévres, where she was welcomed with flowers by the children displaced by war and political persecution housed there. After this dose of harsh reality, Eva hosted an evening reception at the Argentine Embassy for the French authorities where she proudly wore her Legion of Honor. The strain of the trip was taking its toll, and she appeared visibly tired.

Eva's last full day in Paris, on Friday 25 July, began with a special tour of the Palace of Versailles, which was closed to the public while undergoing restoration work. The visit of a First Lady from a wealthy country had a huge impact on the children at a school she called on close to the Bois de Boulogne. Having lived through the deprivations of war, Marc Varangot (then aged 10), remembered: 'We had the impression of receiving a queen who had arrived from another world … [She was] beautiful and dressed in a mink coat … She was introduced to us as a good fairy, which was what they told us at school.'[35] At her last official event, Eva, together with President Auriol, renamed a metro station as Station Argentine in commemoration of the visit and Argentina's support for the French. Eva thanked the press for their kindness during her stay and made a parting donation of 200,000 francs to be distributed to the poor children of the city.

While the Argentine party waited for confirmation of the planned trip to Switzerland, they took the time to travel to Monaco. Eva spent most of her time sunbathing, declining Alberto Dodero's repeated invitations to join him at the casino. She was able to prise herself away from the pool to explore Cannes and Nice and to meet Prince Louis II of Monaco before Ambassador Benito Llambí passed on the official invitation from the Swiss Federal Council. Eva's final destination on the Rainbow Tour would also be her most troubled.

She arrived by train in Geneva on Monday 4 August, from where she was whisked to Parc La Grange for lunch. In the afternoon she left for the Swiss capital, Bern, where she was met by the head of the Ministry of Foreign Affairs, Max Petitpierre, and his wife. The party left the Central Station in two open-top cars bound for the Bellevue Palace Grand Hotel. Within minutes, the car in which Eva was travelling was pelted with tomatoes. Petitpierre gallantly tried to protect his illustrious guest by shielding her body with his. Two young Swiss communists were quickly arrested and Eva laughed off the incident, especially when she saw the state of Petitpierre after the attack. Eva's second day in Switzerland started with a delay when her train to Lucerne broke down. Upon her arrival a more serious incident occurred when the car transporting her to the Municipal Palace was attacked with stones. The first hit the wheel, but the second large stone smashed the windshield, injuring the driver. Eva covered her head with her hands expecting a further onslaught, but a police motorcyclist had run over the assailant before he was able to throw another stone. The perpetrator was quickly identified as a Swiss-Argentine man who had recently been committed to a mental asylum. The Swiss government issued a formal apology for the attacks and hoped the visit would continue without further incident.

One of the more intriguing mysteries surrounding Eva Perón developed during her time in Switzerland. Reports circulated that she had deposited large amounts of money in a Swiss bank account during her visit. In *The Woman with the Whip*, Mary Main claimed that the Eva Perón Foundation kept no records of its accounts, as the foundation was merely a front to allow the Peróns to siphon away millions of dollars. Some believe that this money was for the couple's private use and ultimately paid for Juan Perón's luxurious exile in Spain. Others claim that the money was paid by Nazi war criminals in return for Argentine passports and visas. To organise a tour of Europe with the specific aim of depositing money into a Swiss bank seems like a very convoluted diversion technique. Why wouldn't the presidential couple merely send a trusted advisor to make the deposit? Historians Fraser and Navarro have also countered Mary Main's claims in their discovery that the Minister of Finance, Ramón Cereijo, did keep records of the money used by the Eva Perón Foundation. Investigative journalists and Nazi hunters have searched for a bank account connected to Eva, but so far, none have ever been found to prove these charges.

By accepting the invitation of Ambassador Llambí, Eva extended her stay in the 'Land of milk and honey' by a further two days. She was photographed walking in the mountains of St Moritz with Lillian and members of her Argentine entourage, wearing white trousers and an elegant double-breasted blazer. It was in the resort town that the idea for her autobiography took shape. On Saturday 9 August, during a horse-drawn carriage ride around the lake, Ambassador Llambí told Eva about his conversation with the Spanish journalist, Manuel Penella de Silva, who was interested in writing a book about Eva's life. The First Lady wouldn't meet de Silva until she was back on Argentine soil when they would develop the text that would form the basis of *La Razón de mi vida* (The Reason for my life).[36] Despite having had the idea, and ghostwriting most of the book, de Silva would never be credited for his work. Eva's final day in Switzerland ended with a meal to thank the Argentine staff who had accompanied her on the journey. The event was a mixture of celebration and tears, as it was finally time to return home.

On Sunday 10 August, Eva and her entourage flew to Lisbon and then on to Dakar. There they boarded Alberto Dodero's ship, the *City of Buenos Aires*, for the long journey across the Atlantic. The choice of transportation not only allowed Eva to rest, but also allayed Perón's fears about his wife flying after a recent Argentine plane crash. Before returning to Buenos Aires, Eva had a couple more stops to make on her goodwill tour. First, she was set to represent Perón at the Inter-American Conference for the Maintenance of Continental Peace and Security in Brazil, arriving in Rio de Janeiro on Sunday 17. The following day, Eva's political authority was acknowledged when she was allowed to preside over a congressional session in the Chamber of Deputies. That evening she was awarded the National Order of the Southern Cross during a banquet held in her honour at the at Itamaraty Palace. Eva was treated like a film star during her stay at the Copacabana Palace, where groups of onlookers waited at the gates hoping for an autograph. She was delighted with the renewed attention and must have been looking forward to the welcoming crowds waiting for her in Argentina. The highlight of her stay took place on Wednesday 20 August when she joined the Inter-American Conference to listen to General George Marshall, the American Secretary of State, discuss his 'hemispheric defence' doctrine that would result in the signing of the Inter-American Treaty of Reciprocal Assistance. When Marshall finished speaking, the president of the conference, Raúl Fernandez, introduced Eva as a special guest to the delegations by raising a toast in her name. Eva was not afraid to raise her anti-communist views with the distinguished men in the room and she played the part of ambassadress to the full. Eva's journey homeward continued with a stopover in Montevideo, Uruguay. The visit meant she would arrive in Buenos Aires on a Saturday, which would allow the workers the chance to come and welcome her home. It was the first time that Eva had returned to Uruguay since her theatre tour in 1937. Now, she was the First Lady of Argentina and meeting with the country's President Luis Batle Berres.

The North Dock in the Port of Buenos Aires was resplendent on Saturday 23 August with flags, bunting, and a flotilla of smaller boats and barges, ready to welcome Eva home. Members of the government rubbed shoulders with union leaders, and Eva's mother and sisters as they waited on a raised stage for the return of their First Lady. Just before 3pm that afternoon, Juan Perón arrived with Domingo Mercante as the *City of Montevideo* began mooring. As the other ships in the dock blared their horns in welcome, Eva could be seen on the deck excitingly waving a handkerchief. When she finally stepped ashore, dressed in a Kohinoor mink coat, she was enveloped into a very public embrace by her husband. Perón was proud of her. Eva had been the best representative for his 'New Argentina' that he could have ever wished for. The success of the tour had the effect of silencing the Peróns' critics in Argentina. David Mitchell wrote that 'Most women, whatever their social standing, could not help feeling curiously proud of Eva's audacity. The jokes about the way she'd brushed up her Spanish grammar and taken lessons to try and enlarge her vocabulary, were forgotten.'[37] The woman who hated the rich with such a passion had succeeded in now being received as one of them wherever she went.

The trip, which was initially intended only to last for fifteen days, ended after seventy-nine. It was an unprecedented tour for its time – not just because of the duration, but because it was headed by a female political representative. Eva's mission had been to present Argentina as a strong foreign power in the post-war landscape, and to strengthen economic and diplomatic ties between Argentina and Europe. She had been treated with the deference accorded to a head of state, educated by world-renowned politicians and historians, and adored by (most of) the public. Her self-confidence had increased dramatically as a result. The Rainbow Tour stands as powerful testimony to Eva's use of fashion as a tool of communication: 'As a rainbow, shimmering with a new change of clothes at every appearance, coruscating with glittering jewels, shapely, brown-eyed Eva was unbeatable.'[38] Even though her ostentatious appearance may not have gone down well with those still suffering from the effect of the war, her approach to fashion was extremely successful in Argentina. In relation to her style, there is a clear 'before' and 'after' the Rainbow Tour, and this change in image would be disseminated widely in photographs by the international press.

The trip to Europe transformed her. Gone were the intricate rolled hairstyles and flounced floral dresses, and in their place, she adopted a classic chignon, and incorporated the designs of Dior, Balenciaga and Fath into her wardrobe through New Look style dresses and conservative tailored suits. The evolution of Eva's style embodies the use of clothing and accessories as political tools. To her working-class supporters, she was Cinderella come to life – one of them, but also just out of reach. The Rainbow Tour would be the making of Eva Perón and would forever alter the role of the First Lady in Latin America.

Chapter 6

First Lady Redux
23 August 1947 – 31 December 1949

After her return from Europe, Eva began to acquire a newfound importance within the Peronist regime. The government had been impressed with her conduct and dedication to espousing Peronism on the trip and were confident that she could assume new responsibilities as First Lady. Eva's role as an intermediary between the *decamisados* and her husband, which she believed to be her life's mission, became more established as her social work increased. Once she felt more comfortable in her position of power, Eva was meticulous in the construction of a new image to illustrate her new status. The Rainbow Tour had truly changed how Eva saw the world and how she viewed herself. After being feted like royalty on the trip, she had grown in confidence in her ability to represent the country as their First Lady. This self-assurance therefore needed to be displayed with the use of the European fashions she had fallen for in France and Spain. Eva had noted quite early on in her political life that there were no political wives undertaking the same duties as her that she could emulate. She was therefore free to create a defined style for herself built upon her political knowledge and personal taste. To complete her image transformation, the woman formally known as Doña Maria Eva Duarte de Perón requested that she should be known henceforward as Eva Perón. Her life was now so entrenched with President Perón's, that she had no need for her maiden name.

Eva was, and still is, a woman whose image continues to fascinate. Anticipating the marketing styles adopted by today's influencers, she created her own public image, one that was diffused with and shaped by technology. As Ray Josephs reported:

> By careful use of hairdressers and men, actress Eva Perón has become one of the world's most glamourous – and powerful – women. For today a woman is the dominant figure in the strongest republic in the lower half of the hemisphere. She has the face of a Lana Turner, the figure of a Betty Grable, the radio audience of a Kate Smith and the inexhaustible energy of an Eleanor Roosevelt. That's a large order anywhere. But Evita Duarte de Perón is no ordinary *señora*.[1]

Her confident and attractive image was disseminated through sepia and coloured photographs in newspapers and magazines, official portraits and prints, and in cinema newsreel footage. Her figure was omnipresent in a world where women were gaining more opportunities outside the traditional role of homemaker. Unlike other First Ladies, Eva's entertainment career gave her the advantage of understanding how to communicate with the media. In an era where media interaction still required training, from the start of her public life Eva was able to utilise all she had previously learnt to strengthen her own media presence as well as her husband's. She understood how to use the media to promote images of her devotion to 'her' people, even when controversies raged around her meteoric rise. She articulated her power by dressing as an object of desire, used her unique style of diction when delivering speeches, and radiated charisma to make sure that the image she presented fully supported the narrative she wished to deliver.

The first, and possibly most iconic, change that Eva undertook at this time was to her hair. She would never again appear in public with the elaborate and complicated hairstyles that she had favoured as an actress. She permanently adopted the braided chignon that she had first worn in Europe. The bun at the nape of Eva's neck became symbolic of her authority, with the silhouette giving the illusion of a fist, while also presenting Eva as a woman of purpose who felt self-assured to wear the same, simple hairstyle day after day because her work was her priority. The style was classically timeless and had the added advantage of distinguishing Eva from other women who preferred the popular curled and set hairstyles of the late 1940s. By embracing a signature hairstyle, Eva demonstrated 'discipline, dedication and conviction – all very powerful qualities that reinforce authority'.[2]

Ideology, religion, class and age all contribute to shaping politics, and Eva's Cinderella transformation may have had its roots in her growing maturity. Queen Rania Al Abdullah of Jordan, who herself was thrust into the public eye at a young age, has stated that 'In your 20s, you struggle to identify your look and style. And as this evolves with time, you get comfortable with a style that does not fight with you but enhances you.'[3] Eva became much more intuitive upon her return from Europe in realising that what she wore could be interpreted as a metaphor for her political views. While she had won the adoration of her *descamisados*, she had still yet to prove herself as a woman who was fit to be the wife of the president. To promote a more dignified Eva to the Argentine public, and to further distance herself from her impoverished and illegitimate background, she abandoned the often-flamboyant clothes of her starlet wardrobe in favour of a simpler, more sophisticated image. Her new style utilised the modest luxury fashions of the European couturiers she met in Paris, but kept to Eva's favourite colours of blues, greens and monochrome. By adorning herself in Dior, Balmain and Fath gowns for official occasions, Eva was proving to her doubters that while she could rival any queen, her image would not detract from her work for the poor. Eva explained how 'Like her I am, after all, a woman. I like the same things that she does: jewels and furs, dresses and shoes.'[4] Her new image was a fruitful propaganda tool whose essential objective was to cement Eva in the public consciousness as the ideal representation of Peronist Argentina. Her decision to favour imported European designs over Argentine, was not popular with everyone. Her friend, the designer Paco Jamandreu, was initially hurt by Eva's decision, but had to admit that the styles suited her much better. The two remained close, but Jamandreu would never again be Eva's go-to designer.

Politicians and their spouses must walk a fine line when selecting their wardrobe. Not only must they wear clothes suitable for a leader, they must also dress to please their diverse electorate, articulate an authentic message, and represent their country on the world stage. When this goes wrong, the results can be a PR disaster. Who can forget American First Lady Melania Trump wearing a green hooded Zara jacket with the words 'I really don't care, do u?' emblazoned on the back while travelling to visit detained immigrant children? With her purchasing power, not only did Eva have to represent Argentina as a modern country on the post-war stage through her fashion, she also needed to document the aspiration that elevated her to the top of society. Luxury fashion is frequently criticised as out-of-touch and elitist, yet a large portion of society see it as something unattainable to desire. To the *descamisados* she was seen as a:

> perfect, beautiful perpetual snub to the old snob caste; as the living proof of the inauguration of a new society in which anyone goes and every personable woman has a tiara in her knap-sack. She is one of us, she is our desires fulfilled.[5]

Fashion journalist Robb Young has defined power dressing as 'a matter of what political figures intend to convey with their external image; how their colleagues and the public perceive it; and what it triggers in terms of coming to power, retaining it and governing along the way.'[6] Eva's appeal was able to transcend politics by following these unwritten rules and tweaking them to her own advantage, with the results often eclipsing her husband.

For Eva Perón, her enduring fashion legacy remains with Christian Dior. The year 1947 was a turning point in both their lives. Dior's revolutionary New Look set the course for post-war fashion by representing a return to feminine styles and corseted silhouettes. Eva, whose figure suited Dior's designs, just happened to arrive in Paris at the right time. The couturier and client built a prosperous relationship in which Dior could design for the ultimate diva for whom money was no option, and in return Eva was guided and styled by the 'The Tyrant of Hemlines'. By using haute couture as a political communication tool, Eva became the woman to imitate in Latin America. Magazines and newspapers saw their circulation increase dramatically when they published photographs of her in glamorous haute couture gowns, and her patronisation of Dior was responsible for many ordinary South Americans encountering French haute couture for the first time.

Argentinean women had enjoyed access to European couture since the early decades of the twentieth century. Garments would be shipped across the Atlantic in trunks to be sold in South American outlets of the top couturiers or be delivered directly to a client. All this changed in 1947, when Perón imposed strict import restrictions to defend the industries he had nationalised as part of his first Five-Year Plan. This created an environment of protectionism, fundamentally removing Argentina from competing in the international market. The result of these controls was that clothing imported from Europe became the sole privilege of the First Lady. After the Rainbow Tour, Eva would send her assistant, Asunta Fernández, to Paris twice a year to purchase garments from the new collections.[7] In spring 1949, it was noted that her 'orders included five dresses from Balmain, three each from Dior, Fath and Rochas.'[8] These gowns would arrive in Buenos Aires via ship or in special compartments on Aerolíneas Argentinas

Above: Eva and her siblings dressed for Carnival. (Archivo General de la Nación / Wikimedia Commons)

Right: A teenage Eva showing an awareness of the camera from an early age. (Archivo General de la Nación / Wikimedia Commons)

Eva modelling an improvised blouse and terry cloth suit for the camera of Sivil Wilesnki. (History and Art Collection / Alamy Stock Photo)

Eva's only leading role as Julia in La pródiga (1945). The film was not released until 1984. (Mary Evans / Everett Collection)

The first formal appearance of the presidential couple at the Teatro Colón in July 1946. (Associated Press / Alamy Stock Photo)

Eva's casual appearance in trousers came as a shock to many of members of the upper classes in Argentina. (Dom Slike / Alamy Stock Photo)

Eva visiting the Vatican during her Rainbow Tour, 27 June 1947. (© Illustrated London News Ltd. / Mary Evans)

Above: Eva with Franco and Carmen Polo at the Pardo Palace, Madrid, 9 June 1947. (Album / Alamy Stock Photo)

Below: Eva and Julio Roca (Argentinian Ambassador in France) attending a reception in Paris, July 1947. (Associated Press / Alamy Stock Photo)

Eva in Brazil whilst attending the Inter-American Conference, August 1947. (Mary Evans / Everett Collection)

Above: Eva addressing a crowd of women in 1951. (Pictorial Press Ltd / Alamy Stock Photo)

Below: Eva distributing gifts to children at the Eva Perón Foundation. (Everett Collection / Mary Evans)

Eva and Juan Perón getting ready to attend the Independence Day celebrations in 1950. (Science History Images / Alamy Stock Photo)

Eva and Juan Perón embracing on the Casa Rosada balcony on 17 October 1951. (Dom Slike / Alamy Stock Photo)

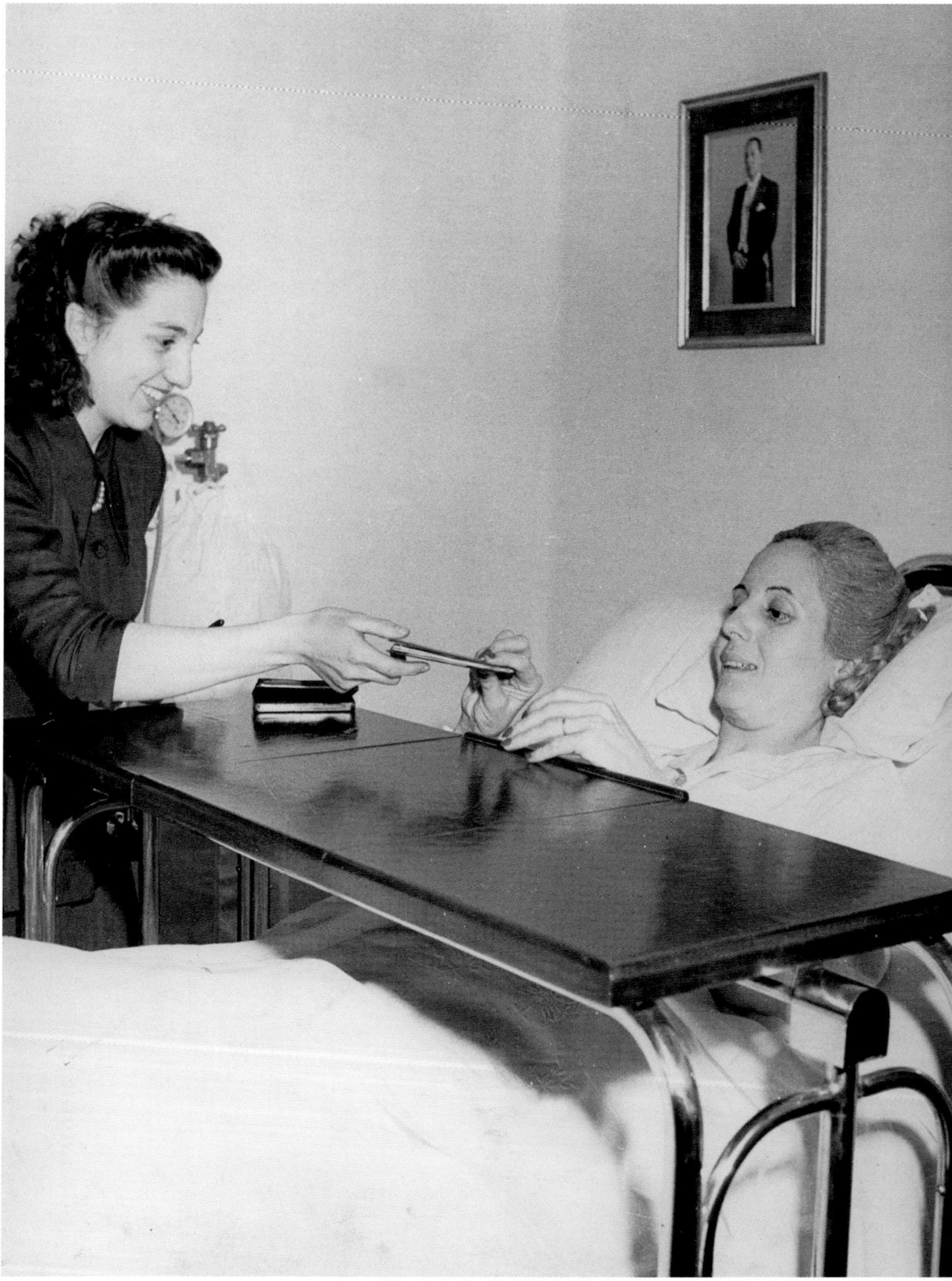

Eva voting for the first and only time from her hospital bed on 11 November 1951.
(Dom Slike / Alamy Stock Photo)

Above: Eva propped up by a frame to ride in an open car alongside her husband for Perón's second term inaugural parade on 4 June 1952. (Everett Collection Historical / Alamy Stock Photo)

Right: The body of Eva Perón lying in state, 1952. (Dom Slike / Alamy Stock Photo)

684—THE ILLUSTRATED LONDON NEWS—October 22, 1955 | October 22, 1955—THE ILLUSTRATED LONDON NEWS—685

THE PERSONAL TREASURES OF GENERAL PERON AND THE LATE SEÑORA PERON: AN EXHIBITION STAGED BY THE ARGENTINE GOVERNMENT, INCLUDING MANY JEWELS.

NOW ABANDONED: WHAT WAS TO HAVE BEEN A FABULOUS MONUMENT TO THE LATE EVA PERON. A HUGE COLLECTION WAS MADE FOR FUNDS TO BUILD IT.

BELONGING TO THE LATE EVA PERON: SOME OF HER MANY FINE FURS AND A DRESS (RIGHT) DESIGNED BY CHRISTIAN DIOR.

GUARDED BY A SOLDIER WITH A SUB-MACHINE-GUN: A DIOR DRESS WHICH WAS SPECIALLY FLOWN FROM PARIS TO BUENOS AIRES FOR EVA PERON.

SCENE OF THE EXHIBITION OF THE PERON POSSESSIONS: THE PRESIDENTIAL RESIDENCE IN BUENOS AIRES, WHERE GENERAL PERON LIVED.

ONLY PART OF THE JEWELS OWNED BY THE LATE EVA PERON: DIAMONDS AND PRECIOUS STONES, WITH (BELOW) GOLD PLATE, CLOCKS AND WATCHES.

PART OF ONE WOMAN'S PERSONAL JEWELLERY: NECKLACES, BROOCHES AND EAR-RINGS OF PRECIOUS STONES BELONGING TO GENERAL PERON'S LATE WIFE.

STATING THAT THE APPROXIMATE VALUE OF THE JEWELS AMOUNTS TO THE EQUIVALENT OF 60,000 WORKERS MONTHLY WAGES: A NOTICE IN THE EXHIBITION.

DISPLAYED IN ORDERLY ROWS: SOME OF THE DRESSES AND SHOES WHICH BELONGED TO EVA PERON AND COST ABOUT £75,000.

COSTING THE EQUIVALENT OF 3,500 WORKERS' MONTHLY WAGES: SOME OF EVA PERON'S NUMEROUS FUR COATS MADE BY THE WORLD'S LEADING FURRIERS.

PRESENTED TO THE LATE EVA PERON: THE "COLLAR OF THE ORDER OF SAN MARTIN," COMPOSED OF GOLD, DIAMONDS AND OTHER JEWELS.

WITH the purpose, presumably, of demonstrating that the ex-dictator of Argentina and his late wife could not properly be regarded as single-minded "friends of the poor," the present Argentine Government, on October 13, exhibited to representatives of the Press a great quantity of jewels, clothing and other possessions of General Peron and the late Señora Eva Peron. The collection was displayed at the Presidential residence in Buenos Aires; and the jewels alone were stated to be worth some £1,250,000. Among other exhibits were 400 suits and dresses, 600 hats and many handbags and pairs of shoes. Some three years ago, soon after the death of Señora Peron, General Peron, it has been recalled, was apparently somewhat conscious of the wealth his wife had amassed, and said that her jewels were "gifts from the people and would be returned to the people." Recently the heirs of an Argentine shipping magnate have claimed that the Perons despoiled them of property to the total value of about £600,000; and they have submitted to the present Government documents which, it is stated, prove this allegation. The exhibition, which was later to be opened to the public, also displayed a quotation from a speech made in July 1954 by General Peron, which may be translated as follows: "There are in every human organization men who work for others and men who work only for themselves. As a rule, things always work out well in an honest man's hands, even if he is not very capable. But God help us if things fall into the hands of a very capable man who, however, has not got much honesty."

Exhibition of Eva's clothes and jewellery that was put on by the Revolución Libertadora after President Perón was deposed. (© Illustrated London News Ltd. / Mary Evans)

Madonna and Jonathan Pryce in Alan Parker's 1996 film adaptation of Evita. (Everett Collection Inc / Alamy Stock Photo)

The enduring image of Eva wearing Christian Dior. (© Keystone Pictures USA/ZUMAPRESS.com/Mary Evans)

planes that allowed the dresses to travel upright on mannequins to avoid creases. When one of these planes was late in arriving with a special dress Eva had chosen to wear for a Gala at the Teatro Colón, the whole performance was delayed by nearly two hours, leaving the audience and performers waiting. Others had to be more creative to circumnavigate the closed borders to compete with the stylish Evita. Designer Bernarda Meneses was one who resorted to smuggling. She would recall how, 'In 1952 I arrived with my brother from Europe bringing twenty-five trunks of clothes. In the Port of Buenos Aires we were received by some posters that said: "Smuggling will be punished with prison".'[9]

One of Eva's first biographers, Mary Main, has speculated about how Eva was able to afford to purchase 'up to a dozen dresses a year from each of the four or five top Paris designers alone, depending on the collections'.[10] Neither she nor Perón had considerable personal fortunes, but Main may have overlooked the fact that Eva was once the highest earning radio star in the country. It is not unfeasible that, due to the company she was keeping, Eva may have been advised to save or invest some of her earnings. She was also lucky enough to receive monetary gifts from Peronist supporters, such as Alberto Dodero, and trade unions and businesses who wished to ingratiate themselves with the powerful First Lady. As Eva was also credited with introducing the designs of Christian Dior, Marcel Rochas and Pierre Balmain to Latin America, it would not be unheard of for such a loyal client who was acting as a walking advertisement to have received discounts or gifts from the couturiers. In any case, we will never know the true extent of Eva's clothing expenses as the bills were burned after the 1955 *coup d'état* that overthrew Perón.

Considering Eva's power and devotion to public work, it is disappointing that the media chose to focus on her appearance more than any other aspect of her life. Unfortunately, it was her influence as a woman that the male-dominated press of the mid-twentieth century frequently resented and chose to ignore or denigrate.

Educated and hardworking royal spouses, including Catherine, Princess of Wales, and First Ladies such as Michelle Obama, are still subject to intense media speculation around their outfits. From the designer label to the cost, and what the style and colour may symbolise, what women in the public eye wear is important. Some have been able to capitalise on this attention to their advantage, or to raise the profile of a certain cause or event. But this scrutiny is also often used to deflect negative attention from male leaders. As women's clothing is obviously more memorable than men's suits, political women are still denounced for excessive spending on fashion, while men are overlooked in our political culture. The fact that a man's tailored suit can cost the same as a woman's designer dress is conveniently ignored.

One of Eva's immediate tasks upon her return from Europe was to secure the passage of the women's suffrage bill through the House of Representatives. She has often been credited with gaining the vote for women singlehandedly, but while she did publish articles and make radio addresses on the subject, the power to enact the law was out of her hands. It is remarkable how the associated propaganda whipped up by the Peronist government has indelibly identified Eva with the legislation. A campaign for women's suffrage had existed in Argentina since the late nineteenth century, but Eva's international reputation as a political figure was seen as having led a movement for social change which in reality had been imposed on Argentina by international forces because the country lagged behind other Latin American countries in granting women the vote.

During the government's campaign, the struggles of past suffragists were conveniently ignored, because Peronist propaganda only looked as far back as the June Revolution in 1943, when the Peronist movement was born. For Juan Perón, the recognition of Argentine women as political citizens was imperative in granting him a decisive re-election in 1951. Ultimately, Perón and Eva were able to capitalise on the passing of the law as their own achievement.

On 9 September 1947, Law 13.010, known as the 'Law of Women's Suffrage', was passed by a large Peronist majority in the Lower House, establishing equal political rights in Argentina for men and women. The enactment of the long-awaited law was celebrated on 23 September in a huge rally organised by the CGT in Plaza de Mayo. Aware of the historical significance, President Perón signed the law in a public ceremony before symbolically handing it to Eva, clearly establishing the myth in the public consciousness that Eva was the main instigator of Law 13.010. The 1947 women's suffrage law profoundly impacted women's lives in Argentina. Having gained the capacity to vote and hold public office, women were able to advocate for better access to education and employment opportunities. As a result, more women began to pursue higher education and to enter traditionally male-dominated sectors, including medicine and law. There was also a huge cultural shift as women's voices became increasingly represented in the media and in literature, helping to break down traditional gender roles and female stereotypes.

The political fairytale brought to life by Juan and Eva Perón was often concealing controversial complexities beneath the glamorous façade. To take full control of the country, the Peronist government needed to wipe out any and all dissent. Press freedoms were severely restricted, the media censored, political opponents jailed and tortured, and critics removed from their positions in the government and education system. University students and professors were particularly vocal in their opposition to Perón. Theologian Herold B. Weiss recalled a popular protest slogan daubed on university buildings in the early 1950s: '*Alpargatas sí, libros no* ('Shoes? Yes! Books? No!'),'[11] which criticised the fact that funding for Eva's social welfare projects often took precedence over education. 1948 was a defining year for Eva's position in Argentina. Her role in the Peronist government began to change, along with her image. The official press started to report more frequently on her participation in solving labour disputes and helping the poor. Eva, already attuned to the language of the media, found that she was able to shine in her new role. Her narrative of small-town-girl-made-good had long been media fodder, and was rightly associated with Peronist 'social justice' victories, both material and symbolic, for the Argentine working class. But this image alone does not explain the extraordinary support she received, or her transformation into the pop culture icon we know today. The legend of Eva Perón was the consequence of social, economic and technological movements taking place in the mid-twentieth century. While on the one hand, she achieved the status of leader through the backing of her devoted *descamisados*, on the other, she was one of the first examples of the 'aestheticisation of politics' in Latin America.[12]

Eva was able to define an era of politics without holding a formal position. The evolution of her image was fundamentally a weapon in her arsenal that allowed her to transform into the queen of the masses. Fashion came naturally to her; it strengthened her image and ignited adoration in others, just as the actresses in her film magazines had done for her as a child. When it was suggested by her advisors that she should tone down her glamorous image, Eva responded: 'the poor like to see me beautiful. How can I let them down?' The Argentine literary and cultural critic Beatriz Sarlo has written widely about her childhood, growing up with a strongly anti-Peronist father. She recalled the impression that photographs of Eva published in her mother's copies of *El Mundo* had on her as a 7-year-old:

> For me, Eva was associated with fashion. I saw her as a model or an actress, even though I knew she was part of the so-called 'regime.' I knew that she worked at the Foundation that carried her name (Peronism was intensely personalistic) and that she 'took care of the poor'. But my eyes were fascinated by the fashion surface. In a way, Eva's beauty had an impact

> on me similar to that which she had on the 'poor'. It wasn't anything they could accuse her of: being an actress, a chorus girl, *a bataclana*.[13] It was an unusual quality in the dull world of political iconography, hitherto dominated by men and, on occasion, as receptions at embassies or patriotic dates, by 40-year-old, heavy, and dull matrons. Eve's youth made her unique. Her beauty made her admirable to those who, like me, were outside and far from politics. She reminded me of movies and fashion magazines.[14]

Her unsavoury past as a second-rate actress faded into the grandeur of her constructed elegance, and through this experience of image transformation as Perón's wife, she metamorphosed into the ultimate representation of the Peronist regime.

For her attendance at the celebrations of the May Revolution at Teatro Colón on 25 May 1948, Eva masterfully embodied her new political image as First Lady by choosing a white silk satin strapless gown, embroidered with pearls and rhinestones on the bust, designed by Jacques Fath. The dress perfectly suited the new sleek silhouette she favoured. Always aware of the symbolism and propaganda involved with her image, Eva chose to be depicted in this gown, which represented purity and transformation, for the official portrait of President Juan Perón painted later that year by Numa Ayrinhac. The fact that this was the first – and only – time that an Argentine president had been accompanied by a First Lady in an official portrait indicates the importance of Eva in the success of her husband.

Eva's dedication to social welfare for her *descamisados* resulted in her greatest achievement as First Lady: the establishment of The María Eva Duarte de Perón Foundation (later shortened to the Eva Perón Foundation) on 8 July 1948. Her work to improve the lives of lower-class Argentines was as much a labour of love as it was a labour of hatred against the wealthy, who she wholeheartedly blamed for the misfortunes of others. The Foundation was Eva's official way of avenging the humiliations of her childhood:

> Take that – higher wages and shorter hours for the workers, for the folk forgotten by the snobs – that's for the hours I fetched and carried, scrubbed and polished, in my mother's boarding-house, and other children in the town were forbidden to play with the *Ibargurens*. Take that – a heavy contribution to the Social Aid Fund, or else that's for all the snubs you've given me, the sneers about my 'artistic' past, about my fitness to be the president's wife. President's wives were supposed to be respectable nonentities.[15]

For Eva, social work was not merely an initiative of a bored First Lady, it was personal. The Foundation's new large warehouse recreated the 'La Tienda de las Delicias' in the garage of the presidential residence on a grand scale and allowed the Foundation to rapidly monopolise the distribution of charitable aid in Argentina, often bringing it into conflict with charities established by the Catholic Church. No one dared question the Foundation, as its charter declared Eva's authority by stating that it was to remain 'in the sole hands of its founder … who will … possess the widest powers afforded by the State and the Constitution'. The charity's main objectives were:

1. To provide with monetary assistance, or in kind, furnish with working tools, give scholarships to any person who lacks resources and requests them, and who, in the founder's judgment, deserves them;
2. To build houses for indigent families;
3. To create and/or build educational establishments, hospitals, homes and/or any other establishments that may best serve the goals of the Foundation;

4. To construct welfare establishments of any kind which can then be given with or without charge to local, provincial or national authorities;
5. To contribute or collaborate by any possible means to the creation of works tending to satisfy the basic needs for a better life of the less privileged classes.[16]

Although Eva generally believed in traditional gender roles for women, she also displayed considerable feminine foresight by understanding that women needed other options of supporting their family, preferably from home. Therefore, the Foundation's purchases harked back to Eva's formative childhood; with 500,000 sewing machines being brought and distributed annually, together with 400,000 pairs of shoes, linens, refrigerators, dentures, wedding dresses, toys and mattresses. Eva personally knew the difference that these items could have on a family. It was the result of her mother Juana's Singer sewing machine that she and her siblings had been able to afford food on the table. 'I remember a letter from a woman to whom I had sent a sewing machine,' Eva would later write. 'She sent me five pesos from her first earnings.'[17] Eva displayed her lived understanding of how learning a trade could make a difference by opening women's Basic Units across the country which offered classes in typing, literacy, sewing and hairdressing. Once educated, women could not only earn an extra income but could also save on their spending by making their own clothes and cutting their family's hair.

Although it was practically unnecessary, Eva would hold audiences three times a week, where she would personally interview applicants for help, distribute money and organise further assistance. A team of social workers and assistants would support her by working their way through the large number of letters that the Foundation received addressed to Eva, responding to each individually and sending packages of requested items. For many people, it wasn't just about receiving aid. It was about receiving Evita. To spend just a few moments in her presence at her office or take delivery of a sewing machine from the woman herself, was like coming face to face with the Lady of Hope. Her work with the Foundation ultimately played a large role in her veneration, leading some to believe her a saint. In 1950, the Catholic poet José Maria Castiñeira de Dios had the opportunity to observe Eva at work. 'She could touch the most terrible things with a Christian attitude that amazed me, kissing and letting herself be kissed,' he remembered. 'There was a girl whose lip was half eaten away with syphilis and when I saw that Evita was about to kiss her and tried to stop her, she said to me, "Do you know what it will mean when I kiss her?"'[18] In the same way that Princess Diana challenged stigma by holding hands with an AIDS patient, through her actions Eva ceased to just be the First Lady and acquired the qualities of a saint.

Amid her gruelling schedule, Eva still found time to open women's shelters, orphanages and schools, and oversee the construction of entire communities such as Evita City[19] in Buenos Aires province, and the miniature Amanada Allen Children's City which offered a refuge for children whose parents were experiencing hardship. Working with the Minister of Health Ramón Carrillo, the Foundation's work to improve medical care in Argentina would lead to equal health care for all for the first time in the country's history. One of the main ways that Eva achieved this was through the creation of the Evita Championships, organised by the Department of Youth Sports of the Eva Perón Foundation. First held in 1948, the Championships were a series of football tournaments for boys held across Argentina, and Eva proudly kicked off the first game dressed in a Marilú Bragance polka dot linen dress and unsuitable heeled shoes. The formation of the Evita Children's Games followed later in the year, and while both were forms of state propaganda aimed at children, they also succeeded in providing young Argentines with access to social sport and medical check-ups.

Within a few years, the Eva Perón Foundation had assets worth in excess of 3 billion pesos and 14,000 employees. During the Peronist government, Eva was conspicuously linked to the Foundation as she began to assume the role of Lady Bountiful, working often up to twenty hours a day and ignoring Perón's requests to decrease her workload. Eva still had to deflect criticism from her opponents, often unaware of her humble background, who condemned her as being out of touch with normal Argentines. She wrote:

> Obviously it would all be absurd if my sharpest-tongued critics were right when they say thoughtlessly that I, 'a superficial woman, uninstructed, common, unacquainted with the interests of her country, remote from the sorrows of her people, indifferent to social justice and with nothing serious in her head, suddenly became a fanatic in the struggle for the cause of the people, and, making that cause hers, decided to live a life of incomprehensible sacrifice.[20]

Eva became almost fanatical in her crusade to eradicate poverty, which is why her decision to wear luxurious fashions often jarred with her aims. During her lifetime, Eva Perón's wardrobe already constituted a matter of state. By dressing like the wealthy women she so openly despised, Eva was the living representation not only of her own upward trajectory, but of the newly won prosperity of the Argentine working-class. She perceived that her supporters wanted their Cinderella to wear Parisian dresses and diamond jewellery because she was the standard-bearer for the masses. Eva would often declare 'I want to look beautiful for my *grasitas*.'[21] Instead of reacting angrily to this ostentatious show of wealth, the *descamisados* applauded her; they recognised that she used designer clothes to portray herself as their queen, someone who had brought about the employment and welfare benefits they now enjoyed.

Eva believed that everyone in Argentina had the right to be rich; in this context, her vanity shouldn't be read as hypocrisy, but rather as a symbol of the higher wages and increased consumer spending which were the result of President Perón's successful economic policies of the late 1940s. Eva also desired that her clothes and jewellery should eventually be put to good use to serve the people:

> With all those belongings, I would like to set up a permanent fund of social aid for cases of collective misfortune that affect the poor, and I would like them to accept it as one more proof of my affection.[22]

Through her Foundation and the adoption of her new image after the Rainbow Tour, Eva had a huge impact upon the nation's popular consciousness. She empowered the Argentine masses as a symbol of triumph over oppression and hardship. The Cinderella fairytale of her life forever changed Argentina's political landscape, by demonstrating that even the most marginalised in society could ascend to the highest spheres of influence by using the system. As journalist Robert Neville observed:

> To Pepe, to the dancer, to the schoolteacher and to the thousands like them, the disinterestedness of Evita's politics and the soundness of her economies are academic issues. She helps. That is enough. Let the wry and witty rich smirk at the propaganda posters that proclaim Evita 'The Madonna of the Humble' and 'The Lady of Hope'. Their laughter never fed a hungry man.[23]

When Juan Perón became president, his main aims were to make the country less reliant on foreign trade and to close the widening gap between Argentina's social classes by increasing employment and workers' pay. In his first two years in office, Perón oversaw the nationalisation of the Central Bank, the railways, public transport and universities. Foreign debts were paid off as Argentina took steps to become more economically independent. Perón also established the Institute for the Promotion of Trade (IAPI), that centralised foreign trade and created a single purchaser for the country's grain exports. Profits resulted in the funding of welfare projects and large wage increases for Argentine workers. Additionally, the Peronist government enacted the Workers' Bill of Rights in 1947 that made access to health care a universal right. Social security was also extended to virtually all members of the Argentine working class. From 1946 to 1951, the number of Argentines covered by social security more than tripled.

Throughout all Perón's work, Eva proved herself to be invaluable. Publicly the loyal First Lady, she was at the same time the more radical of the presidential couple. Eva differentiated herself from former First Ladies by constructing a new profile for women that allowed her to support her husband but also attend to the people for up to fourteen hours a day in what she referred to as her 'afternoons of social assistance'. She served as the de facto minster of Labour and Health, virtually ran the Confederación General del Trabajo, and oversaw her namesake Foundation that had exclusive control over all charitable activity. Eva herself was acutely aware of the dual personality that she presented to the world:

> I had to have a double personality to correspond with Perón's double personality. One Eva Perón, wife of [the] President, whose work is simple and agreeable, a holiday job of receiving honours, of gala performances; the other, 'Evita', wife of the Leader of people who have placed all their faith in him, all their hope and all their love. A few days of the year I act the part of Eva Perón; and I think I do better each time in that part, for it seems to me to be neither difficult nor disagreeable. The immense majority of days I am, on the other hand, 'Evita',

> a link stretched between the hopes of the peoples and the fulfilling hands of Perón, Argentina's first Peronist woman ... There is no need for us to speak of Eva Perón.[24]

Eva's typical day would start at around 7 am at the Unzué Palace with a cup of *maté*. She would then discuss her outfits for the day with Asunta and her maid Irma, before having her hair and nails attended to while her secretary, Atilio Renzi, read through the day's schedule.[25] Once she was at her desk in Perón's former office in the Ministry of Labour, the real work began, meeting delegates from the trade unions. *Life* reporter John Dos Passos was amazed by how Eva's domineering nature with the unions could evaporate if she caught sight of someone she knew in the crowd, 'she'd break away and run up to him with a little schoolgirlish questioning look that said, "Here I am... How do you think I'm doing?" In four hours she never paused or sat down.'[26] In the afternoon, and after a change of dress, she would hold endless audiences with those in need of her Foundation's support before starting her rounds of visits to schools, factories and housing developments. Seldom were Eva's evenings not taken up by an official function of some sort and it was rare that the Peróns were able to dine intimately together. It was also not unheard of for Eva to retire to bed until after 4 am.

As noted earlier, Eva was extremely perceptive to the symbolism of her clothes. A contradiction clearly existed between the dual personality of the glamorous and feminine Eva and the powerful, political Evita. While the couture gowns from Fath and Dior represented Eva Perón and the luxurious side of the Peronist State, for her long workdays when she was Evita, she progressively adopted a pared back image that better reflected her firm desire to be recognised not only as an influential figure, but as a social reformer. In this manner, Eva was symbolically establishing herself as a fashion icon in her new role, alongside Perón's construction of a new Argentina. Clothing by designers Luis D'Agostino and

Luís Manteaux, alongside Dior's tailored skirt suits became her uniform of choice. The suit is perhaps the most traditional example of 'power dressing'. In her seminal book *Sex and Suits*, essayist Anne Hollander described how the suit can become 'the proper material vessel of both beauty and power'.[27]

Eva used the suit to build her identity as Evita, asserting a visual power that she may have felt she lacked because of her gender and upbringing. The suit offered her a form of protection, in that it presented her as a figure of authority accessible and acceptable to both men and women. It also gave her the strength to often be the only woman in the room. The adoption of the suit as her work uniform ultimately reflected her ideological evolution – as her confidence in her role in Perón's administration grew, so too did her style. During her time at the Foundation, Eva accessorised her suits with Argentine leather shoes that were often wider across the foot to make them more comfortable for the long hours she spent on her feet. She also carried the same large bag that is now in the Museo Evita and shows a great deal of wear and tear from frequent use. The widespread image of Eva clad in tailored suits with her chignon hairstyle going about her social work became an enduring image in Argentina's collective memory. To her supporters, the new Evita appeared ready to conquer Argentina and to tackle the problems of her people. Moreover, this was the image that the Peronist government preferred to share when circulating the First Lady's activities.

After Argentine women obtained suffrage in 1947, Eva soon realised that the new law did not guarantee the presence of women as political candidates. Consequently, she founded the Female Peronist Party (PPF) on 29 July 1949 with herself as president. The PPF was organised as an independent party from the male-dominated Peronist Party and excluded the participation of men outright. Units were formed to channel the political participation of women in neighbourhoods and towns into the Peronist movement.

Just as with the male leaders of the Peronist Party, many of the emerging leading members of the PPF were working-class. These units would come to the fore during the economic crisis that hit Argentina in the early 1950s, when they provided free volunteer-led cooking and sewing classes. By 1951, the Female Peronist Party was the largest women's political party in Argentina with 500,000 members. It is strange that while Eva did not consider herself a feminist, her impact on the political lives of women was significant.

Eva Perón was one of the first female political figures to understand politics as spectacle. In her public life, she built up an image to differentiate herself not only from other women, but also from her past. 'I chose to be "Evita" … so that through me the people, and above all the workers, should always find the way open to their Leader,'[28] she would write. As a sartorial emblem of the implementation of female suffrage, Eva adopted the two-piece suit that would become her uniform in her role as First Lady when delegating with the trade unions, and when working twelve-plus hours a day at her social Foundation, keeping her Dior gowns for official occasions. Both images of Eva personified the Argentina Perón wanted to portray to the world and established Evita as a figure of authority. As Ray Josephs would write: 'Her method is an artful blend of showmanship, dramatics, iron nerve and well-dressed sex appeal. She has the look of a clotheshorse and a mind that is bright and hard. Her rise to power sounds like an accident in history; a Cinderella story with a Latin twist.'[29] Her transformation into Evita was complete.

Chapter 7

The Good Fairy
1 January 1950 – 31 December 1951

No other woman in 1950 held as much power through the force of her personality than Eva Perón. But for the woman who offered her body as the ideal image of the Peronist regime, the fact that her health would be the downfall of everything she had worked for was incomprehensible. Eva had always been physically fragile, and on the 9 January 1950, she fainted in public during an official function. She complained of stomach cramps and was diagnosed with appendicitis, for which she underwent an appendectomy performed by Dr Oscar Ivanissevich. Eva struggled to recover from the operation and was left exhausted due to the anaemia caused by vaginal bleeding. She refused to undergo any further treatment in case it interfered with her demanding work schedule.

Eva's health was of international importance, especially to Argentina's critics. The British Ambassador in Buenos Aires, Sir John Balfour, sent a letter to the head of the American Department in the Foreign Office reporting on the gossip circling around Eva's health. He told Sir Alfred Stanley Fordham that 'I think you should know that rumours are going the rounds to the effect that Mme. Perón's condition is more serious than is generally believed.'[1] Balfour relates how the French *Chargé d'affaires*, Senor Monmayou, was of the opinion that Eva had been treated by a gynaecologist and not a surgeon, and that the official diagnosis of appendicitis was in fact a lie. Dr Ivanissevich would later claim that it was during the appendectomy that he diagnosed Eva with the cervical cancer that would ultimately claim her life. This story was never verified, but Monmoayou's information sounds like it may have come from a source close to the doctor. Balfour concluded his letter by acknowledging the hold Eva had over Argentina; 'any serious deterioration of the *Señora's* health would have such incalculable effects here that I feel I should let you know what people are saying in this connection.'[2] The true feelings of most of the British foreign office towards Eva was captured in a single line of the minutes: 'Whatever the truth of these rumours, nothing but good could result from a prolonged spell of ill health.'[3]

The fairytale image of the dashing president and his beautiful First Lady was not to everyone's taste. Peronism was viewed by many countries as a totalitarian ideology, with Juan Perón often being compared to the fascist dictators who had inflicted the Second World War on the world. The three flags that define the ideal of Peronism: economic independence, social justice and political sovereignty, were criticised by opponents as populist policies. By rejecting the interference of other countries in Argentina's domestic affairs, and focusing on promoting national industry, countries such as Britain found themselves suddenly excluded by their close trade partner. After the Rainbow Tour, Perón's government became focused on silencing internal opposition and often turned to violence to quieten dissenters, who were accused of being unpatriotic. Socialists accused Perón of enflaming class division, Liberals denounced his use of dictatorial powers, and Conservatives hated his modernist ideas. Juan Perón preferred to suppress critics, who came from both the left-wing and conservative factions, by removing their access to print media. Since taking power, the Peronist Party had purchased majority shares in publishing houses, closed or seized companies, installed Peronist supporters in positions of powers, or resorted to intimidation to censor the Argentine press. The creation of the state's own media company, The Asociación de Loterías Estatales de Argentina (ALEA), provided the government with their own personal outlet to publish favourable propaganda to the masses.

Eva would not allow her declining health to hold her back from fulfilling her duties and refused repeated appeals from her advisors to decrease her workload. By 1950, the Eva Perón Foundation was larger than some governmental ministries, controlling hospitals, schools, housing, parks, children's homes and a chain of retail stores. With the social aid warehouse alone now occupying ten floors, and the headquarters based in an imposing neoclassical building on Avenue Paseo Colón, Eva needed to be in the thick of the action to ensure her wishes were being carried out. Her face smiled back at Argentines from posters promoting the Foundation and directing them to make any request, big or small. As *Illustrated* reported, 'If you are poor and need a pair of shoes, if you are a little girl dreaming of owning a doll with real hair and eyes that open and close – what should you do? You must know about the Good Fairy.'[4] Aged 9, Beatriz Sarlo was hit by a truck while playing outside her local church and spent months in hospital. At Christmas, gifts started to arrive at the hospital from the Eva Perón Foundation that were to be distributed to the children with Eva's photo. The little girl was immediately smitten with the lady in the photo, who the nurses assured her was thinking of all the ill children. For Sarlo, whose father viewed Eva as nothing more than a prostitute, her experiences with the Foundation led her to question what she had been told about the First Lady. Eva herself was aware of the importance of a woman's morals and advised the girls that her Foundation assisted, to: 'Be careful! Be irreproachable in your behaviour and your manners. Dress elegantly. I made mistakes, but I was saved because I am Perón's wife. But for you, any false step, and they'll be all over you.'[5]

To fund the ever-growing Foundation, Eva needed money, and quickly. The trade unions were big donors, along with businesses who knew that refusing to contribute may result in fines or even closure. One method that Eva concocted to finance the Foundation was achieved by using her power to encourage the Ministry of

Labour to pass a resolution in October 1951 enjoining all employers to retain two days' wages of each of their employees as a 'contribution' to the Eva Perón fund. Not all workers were happy, but there were no public demonstrations of their dissatisfaction. The Ministry stated that the resolution had been adopted at the request of the General Confederation of Labour, and as it was extracted without the approval of Congress, many, including the British Embassy in Argentina, believed that it indicated that 'the Senora is determined to use every possible means to lay her hands on a large and stable source of income for her fund'.[6]

Even though the Foundation became her life's mission, another side of Eva Perón was captured by the American writer and editor Fleur Cowles. Cowles and her third husband, publisher Gardner Cowles, Jr., were granted an audience with the Peróns during a 5½-day trip they undertook to Argentina in May 1950. The short encounter between Eva and Fleur Cowles formed the basis of Cowles' 1951 book, *Bloody Precedent*, that compared the Peróns to the nineteenth-century Argentine political power-couple, Manuel and Encarnacion de Rosas. Cowles' first glimpse of the First Lady about whom she had heard and read so much came as something of a shock:

> She was not at all the allegedly over-dressed hussy; not at all the flashy companion old news accounts prepared you for … She was elegantly dressed in a navy-blue suit by Jacques Fath; she had an expensive navy-blue beret on her blonde hair. There were sables on her arm; she wore them as if she had always carried them. She was dressed as millions of women would like to be dressed. The only giveaway was the orchid in her lapel. No real flower that, but one of diamonds, larger even than an orchid, about five inches across by seven inches high – a brooch of big, pure white diamonds that must have been worth $250,000.[7]

The two women shared several traits, not least their blonde hair, love of fashionable clothes and advantageous marriages. Both were also ambitious hard workers, with Cowles telling *Time* magazine, 'I've worked hard, and I've made a fortune, and I did it in a man's world, but always, ruthlessly, and with a kind of cruel insistence, I have tried to keep feminine.'[8] It is possible that the similarities the women saw in each other meant that they didn't hit it off.

Even though the women spent less than a week in each other's company, Cowles claims that Eva was keen to talk 'girl talk' with her, discussing jewellery, clothes and which hairstyle Cowles thought suited Eva best. Cowles presents Eva as quite a lonely figure whose work was her life, but her 'sudden childlike change from queen to mere woman'[9] displayed a need to chat and gossip with another like-minded woman. Cowles was witness to the full force of Eva's love of glamour when the First Lady invited the journalist to accompany her to a rally at the Teatro Colón. Eva had previously been coy when answering Cowles' questions about what made her happy, but that evening, when the crowds spotted Eva arriving at the theatre, Cowles observed how they surged towards her 'to touch her skirt, to see, at close hand, the Cinderella dressed by Dior, with her three-quarters of a million dollars in jewels'.[10] As Eva acknowledged her supporters, she turned and winked at Cowles. The adoration of her people was what made her happy.

Eva's adoption of the full-skirted evening gowns from the ateliers of Christian Dior and Marcel Rochas embodied her desire to dress the part of a 'professional Cinderella' that her supporters feted. In her book, Cowles described Argentina as being shrouded in a 'Petticoat Curtain', with Eva as the de facto power behind the throne, because these gowns also had the symbolic effect of marking out Eva as usually the only woman in a group of men, and for making it necessary for her to be one step ahead of the men to avoid their treading on her skirts.

In 1950, Eva spent more than $40,000 on clothing from Parisian couturiers, and Cowles was suspicious (if not also a little jealous) of how she could afford it. When Perón had taken Cowles' columnist Harlan Miller on a tour of the Unzué Palace, the president had commented on Eva's bursting wardrobes (that were said to take up multiple rooms in the presidential palace): 'Not exactly a *descamisada*, eh?'[11]

During an interview, Cowles was able to ask Eva directly about the approximately $100 million that the Eva Perón Foundation acquired every year. Cowles was well aware of the allegations around the misappropriation of funds and the American government's unease around what they perceived as Eva's socialist support for the unions and the poor, and wanted to get to the bottom of how such a vast amount of money was carefully managed. It turned out it wasn't. Eva honestly admitted that no accounting books were kept for the charity. 'I just use the money for the poor,' she told Cowles. 'I can't stop to count it.'[12] *Bloody Precedent* was published in 1951, and while it depicts Juan and Eva Perón as stereotypical despots, it also presents a more vulnerable and human side to Eva as a woman who often found herself isolated in the male dominated world of politics.

The edition of *Life Magazine* on 11 December 1950 presented to the world the image we most closely associate with Eva Perón – the Dior-clad 'Good Fairy'. The photographs taken by German-born French photographer Gisele Freund were first featured in the British publication *Illustrated* in September 1950, but reached a wider audience through the *Life* photo-report entitled 'Eva Perón: A First Look at the Private Life of a Controversial First Lady'. Freund was best known for her documentary style photographs, often focusing on candid portraits of writers and artists, such as Virginia Woolf and Frida Kahlo. After settling in Argentina in the early 1940s, she began working as Magnum Photos Latin America contributor from 1947. She approached her intimate study of Eva

Perón by formulating a narrative around the social construction of femininity. She photographed Eva in the presidential residence brushing out her long blonde hair, having her nails varnished, and getting ready to begin a sixteen-hour day at the Foundation. Eva is also shown alongside her maid Irma, in the 'three large rooms, lined with immense cupboards, [that] are needed to house her furs, suits, hats and shoes',[13] selecting the strapless sky-blue embroidered tulle Christian Dior *Bach*[14] evening dress and matching feather cape that she would wear at the Teatro Colón to attend the celebrations for Argentina's national holiday on 9 July. President Perón's amused response to his wife's couture ensemble was 'You look like an ostrich!'

For the presidential couple's supporters, the press and official photographs of their republican queen dressed in her European couture gowns and Perón in his dress uniform were a source of pride. 'To many a *descamisado*, *Señora* Perón is Cinderella come to life, and should she not dress accordingly?' asked Robert Neville in *Life Magazine*.[15] The Peróns could rival the glamour and elegance of royalty, and photos of the pair attending formal events were known to increase the sales of the newspapers and magazines that printed them. These photographs were the prevailing representation of Eva's rise from humble origins to the top of Argentine society and, together with those depicting Eva as a saint, have remained the favoured images displayed in the homes of Peronists up to this day. Formal photographs of 'that woman', as her critics disparagingly referred to Eva, were also the best representation of the president's wife for her opponents, depicting what an unknown young woman could achieve by becoming the mistress of a powerful man – respectability, and the total subversion of the Argentine class system.

What Eva wore was also imitated across South America and the wider world. Her style gave the world a reason to know and care about Argentina. The biggest compliment she received was when an Italian interviewer asked Christian Dior about his clients, and the couturier replied: 'The only queen I dressed was Eva Perón.' Eva's adoption of European couture did, however, lead to a wasted opportunity in her role as First Lady. Even though she wore garments from Argentine designers, she was so transfixed with following international trends in order to compete with the upper classes that she failed to encourage and promote the Argentine fashion industry. The import regulations of the period, together with the internal migration that took place in Argentina, created what would have been ripe conditions to encourage growth in the textile industry. Sociologist Susana Saulquin has attributed a number of factors to Eva's failure to create a national fashion identity. First, Eva did not have the time to focus her energy on Argentina's textile industry. Second, and most important, Eva used her clothes as political weapons and 'in her desire to compete with the upper class, instead of generating a style, she appropriated it'.

By 1950, state functions and receptions were one of the few times when the presidential couple still spent time together. Even though Eva enjoyed the opportunities to wear the beautiful gowns and jewellery that these functions afforded her, she had become increasingly disillusioned with the time the events took her away from her social work. During the final years of her life, when her power was at its peak, she spent most of her time as the people's 'Evita' in her conservative working wardrobe of a tailored suit, but the image that remains in the public consciousness today is that of the glamourous Eva Perón. Gisele Freund's decision to focus her narrative in *Life Magazine* on Eva's image creation through the time and money spent on her beauty regime and ostentatious wardrobe, alongside the work undertaken at the Foundation, presented Eva as a new type of woman. She could work, be politically active, fashionable, feminine, and respectful of her position as a wife. This was in stark contrast to the conservative American ideal of the housewife. The photos ultimately resulted in a diplomatic row between Argentina and the United States. The Argentine government claimed the photograph negatives were sent abroad without their official permission – but the more likely reason may have been that Perón's supporters were unhappy with Freund's focus on the Peróns' ostentatious lifestyle, which contradicted the party line on social inequality. In the end, *Life Magazine* was no longer distributed in the country and Freund had to leave Argentina.

Even as her health declined, Eva was still very much involved in national and international politics. Her love of celebrity also never went away, and when she heard that Oscar-winning actress Joan Fontaine was in Argentina for a State-Department sponsored publicity tour, she arranged an audience with the star. Fontaine had initially balked at the idea, but agreed to a private meeting with Eva after her passport was withheld. The following day she was escorted around Eva's social projects before being driven to the Ministry of Labour. After being made to wait for over half an hour, Fontaine was eventually ushered into Eva's office. The First Lady began their conversation by expressing her love of the movies, stating 'People say we look alike. I think so, too.'[16] When Eva asked Fontaine for advice about navigating the public eye, the actress was brutally honest. Citing Eva's ostentatious display of wealth on the Rainbow Tour while some in Europe still had little to eat, 'I said she would have been far more welcome if she'd brought wheat and beef, two of the principal Argentine exports, instead of empty splendour.'[17] Eva listened quietly – she understood. Fontaine remarked 'She was an excellent propagandist in her own country, as President Perón well knew.'[18]

Eva additionally took centre stage during a state visit to Argentina made by Prince Bernhard of the Netherlands in early April 1951. The husband of Queen Juliana was received by the president and the First Lady, and taken on visits to the Eva Perón Foundation, the Metropolitan Cathedral, and to army barracks to see Perón's prized collection of horses. To thank the prince for his much-publicised visit, Juan Perón awarded Bernhard with the Order of Liberator,

San Martín. In return, Prince Bernhard decorated Eva, not Perón, with the Grand Cross of the Order of Orange-Nassau. There is always a business and political element to any state visit, and historian Norberto Galasso has claimed that the visit came about after Perón ordered a large number of guns from the prince to be given to the *descamisados* in case there was a military coup. The Dutch government then purportedly saw an opportunity to bribe Perón into building a railway for them. Whether Prince Bernhard was aware of the dubious deal is not known. But as he would later become embroiled in the 'Lockheed Bribery Scandal', it seems more likely than not.

On 9 April, only days after Prince Bernhard had left Argentina, Eva held a meeting with the Minister for Labour for the new country of Israel. Golda Meir's visit may seem strange considering Juan Perón infamously allowed many Nazi war criminals to take refuge in Argentina after the end of the Second World War. What is perhaps less known is that Argentina also welcomed more Jewish immigrants into the country than any other in Latin America and is now home to the largest population of Jewish citizens in South America. Juan Perón was an extremely complicated man and although antisemitism existed in Argentina, Perón himself worked closely with the Jewish Peronist organisation, the *Organización Israelita Argentina* (OIA). The nationalism that was an essential part of Peronism embraced all races (which had previously excluded indigenous peoples, such as Juan Perón's own mother). He even appointed several Jewish Argentineans to government roles. Argentina's relationship with Israel began to grow closer from 1949, when Eva had started sending containers of humanitarian aid to the country through her Foundation. Meir later wrote about her meeting with the president and Eva, declaring that she embraced Eva for the work she did in favour of the state of Israel.

The publicity generated around Eva's roles in these important state visits all helped with the campaign to promote Eva as Perón's candidate for vice president at the next elections. For the first time, Eva sought to establish for herself a legitimate political role within Perón's government. While the role of vice president wouldn't have granted Eva much constitutional authority, it would have nevertheless represented the next step to the presidency. As vice president, if Juan Perón was to die in office, Eva would succeed him. It was this possibility that angered many of Eva's opponents, especially within the military, who deplored her strengthening powers in the government. Slogans such as '*Viva Perón Viudo!*' (Long Live Perón the Widower) and '*Viva el cáncer*' (Long Live cancer) appeared daubed on walls across the country. Eva's charismatic personality, and the faith she held in the power of her supporters to protect her from her critics, helped to insulate her from the personal attacks meted out by her critics. She naively believed that this time would be no different. Eva's popularity, particularly among working-class women, would be a huge asset to Perón and made up his mind to choose his wife as his running mate. He was also becoming more aware of how Eva's stature within the Peronist party now rivalled his own. On account of this historical political move, Eva was featured with Perón on the cover of the 21 May 1951 edition of *Time* magazine.[19] Ernest Baker's life-like illustration positions Eva in front of her husband in a slight suggestion of who was really running the country.

For the 141st anniversary celebrations of Argentina's Independence in May 1951, Eva pulled out all the stops. Believing that she would be the country's new vice president before the end of the year, she cemented her rags-to-riches story by choosing to wear Christian Dior's *Amérique* evening gown. The fairytale gown made from silk satin and tulle and studded with sequins was the ultimate 'princess' dress. The gown will forever be culturally identified with Eva, not only as a symbol of Argentina's wealth at the time, but also of Eva's femininity. It has been recreated countless times for the lead actress to wear to perform *Don't Cry for Me Argentina* in stagings of Evita, and a version was even made by Dior for Argentine-raised actress Anya Taylor-Joy to wear on the red carpet at the 2024 Cannes Film Festival. The showstopping nature of the gown, worn on the night with an embroidered Dior evening coat of pale pink satin, connoted royal imagery that instilled a sense of national pride among her supporters. Biographer Mary Main described the impact that Eva had – even on her detractors – when she was at her 'most beautiful':

> I saw her first at her most beautiful. It was at a gala performance at the Colón Opera House and I stood in the crowds … and she came, a slender, pale-haired, dark-eyed woman passing with the swiftness of flight, her spreading dress and satin cloak all rose, embroidered gold and deeper rose. She paused a moment to shed her smile this way and that, and then sped on, the president and all his ministers at her heels.[20]

She quickly followed this iconic gown with another, when she wore Marcel Rochas'[21] strapless black velvet and silk taffeta *Siréne Noire* evening dress for the Independence Day gala on 9 July 1951, and for official photographs by Pinélides Fusco.[22] Marcel Rochas was known as something of a ladies man 'who charmed his models, his clients, his female friends, and even celebrities'.[23] Eva Perón became a client in the early 1950s when Rochas, who was fascinated by South American culture, explored the continent for ideas to incorporate into his designs.

On 22 August 1951, the CGT organised a huge rally to promote the Perón-Perón ticket in the Avenida 9 de Julio. Juan and Eva addressed the crowds from a vast scaffold stage that had been constructed in front of the Ministry of Public Works. It has since been claimed that the '*Cabildo Abierto*', as the rally was called, was the largest public display of support for a female political figure in history, with over a million people in attendance. An emotional Eva began her speech to the masses by evading accepting the candidacy for vice president. The crowds insisted that she make a decision, and an intense dialogue started between the people and the First Lady. Eva asked for time to think things over, stating 'I do not renounce my work, I only renounce the honours', but the crowds continued to chant '*Ahora, Evita, ahora!*' ('Now, Evita, now!'). President Perón may have been disconcerted by the strength of the support shown for his wife, and Eva was forced to step away from the microphone. When she returned later that night she proclaimed 'Friends! As General Perón said, "I will do as the people ask."' The crowds cheered, believing that she had finally accepted the role of vice president. The following day, Eva collapsed from severe abdominal pain. Although her diagnosis was withheld from her, she must have known that she was seriously unwell and that seeking the vice presidency was no longer practical.

Less than a week later, Eva shocked her supporters by making a nationwide radio broadcast announcing her decision to renounce the candidacy:

> I want to tell the people of Argentina my definitive and irrevocable decision to decline the honour that the workers and the people of my country wished to honour me with at the historic *Cabildo Abierto* [Open Town Council] on 22 August … I did not have then, nor do I have right now, more than one ambition, only one, great personal ambition: That my people may say, when this wonderful chapter of history is written and surely dedicated to Perón, that at the side of Perón, there was a woman who was dedicated to bringing to the president, the hopes of the people. Hopes that which later, Perón would convert into beautiful realities. And this woman, the people lovingly called Evita – nothing more than this, Evita.[24]

In Peronist folklore, this moment became known as 'The Renunciation', portraying Eva as embodying the feminine value of self-sacrifice that was an ideal within *marianismo* in Hispanic American culture. The reasons for Eva's renunciation are still not fully known. Was there just one cause that forced her to renounce her political career? Or was it a combination of factors that ranged from the military's opposition to her, the rising power of the CGT in Argentina, President Perón's concerns about his wife's power, her worsening health, or even the personal decision of the First Lady herself to step aside?

In late September, biopsy results finally correctly diagnosed Eva as having cervical cancer. Father Hernán Benítez, who was with President Perón when Eva's doctors told him of the advanced state of the cancer, would later recall that 'this blow struck Perón as hard as anything he had ever experienced'.[25] After losing his first wife, Aurelia, to the same cancer, Perón was acutely aware of the pain and suffering that was to befall Eva. For Perón, his life would never be the same again. He would never tell his wife the truth about her illness. Whether this was because he feared her diagnosis would overshadow his re-election campaign, or because he felt guilty knowing that he may have transmitted the fatal HPV virus to both of his wives, we may never know. Gynaecologist Dr Jorge Albertelli was hired to cure the First Lady and moved into the presidential residence to be closer to his patient. On 27 September Albertelli began treating Eva with radium, then a standard therapy for cancer treatment. The doctor was amazed by the physical and emotional strength of Eva when a failed *coup d'état* against Perón, led by General Benjamin Menéndez, took place the following day. Instead of following medical advice to rest, Eva took to the microphone to respond to the events with a speech on the radio thanking the *descamisados* for standing by their president and asking God to return her to full health so she could continue the fight.

Eva had fought too hard to get to her position to let her health stand in the way. On 17 October 1951, the sixth anniversary of her first appearance on the Casa Rosada balcony, Eva roused herself from her sickbed to speak to her *descamisados*. The woman who stepped out on to the balcony was a far cry from the glamourous Eva of the 'Rainbow Tour'. Dressed in a classic dark suit with her hair pinned back into the iconic chignon, she looked tired and emotional throughout the ceremony. Juan Perón, foreseeing that this may be his wife's final Loyalty Day, feted Eva by declaring 17 October to be 'Santa Evita Day'. She was presented with two medals on the balcony. The first on behalf of the CGT, and the Great Peronist Medal in Extraordinary Degree from her husband on behalf of the country. The event was the first to be shown on live television after Jamie Yankelevich worked with the Peróns to create Argentina's first state-owned television station, Televisión Pública. The president was captured speaking about his wife in public for the first time. In an almost funereal speech about the woman standing beside him, Perón spoke of how, 'With her natural capability of organising politically on a mass scale, she has given the Peronist movement a new orientation and a mystique.' He praised her work with the trade unions and in founding the Female Peronist Party. Eva was stunned by Perón's public declaration of gratitude. She was able to give a short speech to the crowds in which she declared:

> it is certain my wish is that I will soon be back in the struggle, with more strength and love, to fight for this people which I love so much, as I love Perón. And I ask you just one thing: it's certain I will soon be with you, but if for health reasons I am not, take care of the general. Remain faithful to Perón as you've been until today, because this means being loyal to the Fatherland and loyal to yourselves. And to all the *descamisados* of the interior, I hold them closely, so very closely to my heart, and want them to know how much I love them.[26]

Crying and visibly shaking, Eva turned from the crowds and embraced Perón in an image that brought tears to the eyes of the toughest *descamisados*.

Much like the media speculation around the health of Catherine, Princess of Wales, in 2024, there were those who believed that Eva was only pretending to be ill. The military's frustration with Eva's candidacy was well known, and some people truly thought that she was only faking her illness to give her an excuse to travel to Switzerland on the pretext of recuperating. Once settled, Juan Perón would then join her, and the couple could live off the millions they had allegedly ciphered away from the Eva Perón Foundation into a supposed secret Swiss Bank Account. An account has never been proven to exist and the claims only help to illustrate Eva's exceptional capacity for inspiring, as well as manufacturing, myths.

By November, it had become clear that Eva's health was deteriorating rapidly. The Perón government declined to disclose the nature of her illness, and conflicting press reports debated whether she had cancer. The radium implants being administered proved futile and Eva became extremely weak from acute vaginal bleeding, which often necessitated her changing clothes numerous times in a day. Her physicians decided it was time to operate in an attempt to eradicate the cervical cancer. Argentina's eminent oncologist, Dr Abel N. Canónico, was consulted, and he recommended the American surgeon and pathologist George T. Pack of the Memorial Sloan-Kettering Cancer Center to perform the surgery. Canónico flew to New York to discuss Eva's case with Pack before escorting him back to Buenos Aires, whereupon the Argentine government announced that the First Lady would be undergoing an unspecified operation. On 6 November, Eva underwent a radical hysterectomy at her Foundation's Avellaneda Polyclinic Hospital. President Perón and Eva's family requested that she not be told of Canónico or Pack's involvement, as they did not want to distress her or to alert the populace during the presidential campaign. Therefore, George Pack operated in secret, only entering the operating theatre after Eva had been anesthetised and leaving before she regained consciousness. During the surgery, Pack found that the cancer had metastasised to adjacent pelvic organs. There was not much more he could do.

On 11 November, only five days after her surgery, Eva voted for the first and only time in a general election. A ballot box was brought to her hospital bed as she recuperated, the moment was photographed and disseminated widely in the press. The results of the election were close to her heart, as not only was President Perón re-elected, but nearly 4 million newly enfranchised female voters exercised their right to vote, with 63.9 per cent doing so in favour of the ruling Peronist Party.[27] Achieving the right to vote had been the first challenge to overcome, but convincing Argentine women to cast their vote on election day was another entirely. Through the efforts of Eva and the Female Peronist Party, women from all social classes and professions were represented at the polling booths, and more impressively, twenty-three female representatives, six senators and eighty legislators were elected to governmental positions. This huge achievement aided Eva's recovery and her conviction to resume political activities.

The year ended with the publication of Eva's unashamedly propagandist autobiography, *La Razón de mi vida (The Reason for my Life)*. Spanish journalist Manual Penella da Silva was initially approached in 1950 to write a memoir for Eva, but his finished manuscript was heavily criticised by Juan Perón and members of the government. Perón gave the text of what would become *La Razón de mi vida* to his speechwriter Raúl Menda, who reworked the book with the involvement of the Perón regime, ultimately removing a chapter analysing Eva's political contributions. This is the version of the book still available to this day. Upon its initial publication, the book was illustrated with images of Eva in her couture gowns and jewels, but this was quickly withdrawn as it no longer represented the political image that Eva or the government wanted to convey. A new edition was published that depicted Eva in her working uniform of tailored suits, with a frontispiece portrait by Numa Ayrinhac showing Eva in a dark blue Marcel Rochas dress with a silk rose corsage.

It is extraordinary how the political power that Eva wielded only seemed to increase as her physical health declined. Her image was undergoing one final symbolic transformation – into that of the Peronist Saint.

Chapter 8

Spiritual Leader of the Nation 1952

The year 1952 began with an award ceremony for the 'Master of Argentine surgery', Dr Ricardo Finochietto at the presidential residence on 4 January. He was decorated for his treatment of the First Lady, who appeared back to full health as she posed beside him for photographs wearing a cream and black linen Jacques Fath dress embellished with rhinestones. She spent some time in the new year on the presidential yacht and even felt well enough to attend the Epiphany celebrations at the presidential residence where she gave out gifts to children, but her public appearances were dwindling. Juan and Eva Perón's meeting in February that year with the famous French boxer, Georges Carpentier, 'produced one of Eva Perón's now rare public appearances in Buenos Aires. Mme. Perón – well groomed as ever, but noticeably thinner since her illness last November – smiled as her husband, the Argentine president, linked arms with 'Gorgeous George'.[1] Even though Eva continued to undergo radiotherapy treatment, a biopsy taken later that month revealed that her cervical cancer had spread to her lungs, and her medical team quickly decided against further surgery. Instead, her doctors arranged for Eva to become one of the first Argentines to undergo chemotherapy with nitrogen mustard to try and relieve the symptoms of chest pain and a cough with which she suffered.

Eva Perón delivered her last public speech on 1 May, Labour Day in Argentina. Struggling to stand on the balcony of the Casa Rosada, Juan Perón was photographed supporting Eva at the waist. She used her final address to rally against her enemies. She urged the people to fight against anyone who disagreed with Peronism, namely the oligarchy who she had detested since her childhood. Her incendiary tone represented a new violence in her devotion to Perón. Whether because of her medication, her pain, or the fact that she knew she was dying, she attacked enemies of Perón by declaring:

> If it is necessary, we will execute justice with our own hands. I ask God not to allow these madmen to raise their hands against Perón, for beware of that day when I will go down with the working people, I will go down with the women of the people, I will go down with the *descamisados* and I will leave nothing standing that is not for Perón.

Exhausted by her aggressive rhetoric, she had to be carried back inside by Perón who realised, 'In my arms, there was nothing more than a dead woman.'[2]

Eva was able to publicly celebrate her 31st birthday on 7 May 1952, even though she was in fact 33. Congress awarded her with the official title of 'Spiritual Leader of the Nation', and presented her with the sole Extraordinary grade Order of the Liberator General San Martín. In a rare and touching moment during the presentation of the unique gold and platinum collar, President Perón openly embraced his wife. These tributes recognised Evita's importance to the history of Argentina and possibly afforded Perón a way to publicly thank his wife for her constant support without admitting the truth about her health. The jewelled collar, made up of 753 precious stones, would be the finest and the final piece of jewellery that Eva would acquire into her personal collection.

Even as her health rapidly declined, Eva's need to keep up appearances by looking beautiful was still evident. Whether her hope of wearing a glamourous gown fuelled her need to survive, or if she just couldn't do without the latest fashions, she continued to make regular purchases with European fashion houses, and a client statement exists from Christian Dior dated as late as 13 May 1952.[3] When these garments arrived from Europe, Eva was so thin that she was unable to wear them and asked her maids Pilar and Irma to model them for her while she rested in bed with her poodle Canela. The physical toll that the cancer was taking was illustrated by Eva's sister Erminda, who noted that when Eva's clothes were first lent to the Museo Evita the linings were found to be soaked in perspiration and needed cleaning professionally before going on display. Eva's extreme weight loss may have put an end to her spending as she began to re-wear more of her clothes instead. She invited Paco Jamandreu to take apart and alter her clothing,[4] which also offered Eva the opportunity to spend time with her close friend. Eva's style evolution mirrored the changing moments of her life. She consciously shaped her image to suit her situation, leading her confessor, Father Benítez, to state that her love of clothes and jewels would hinder her chance of ever becoming a saint. As she neared the end of her life, Eva was head to say, 'If God gives me back my health, I will never wear jewels or beautiful dresses again. Nothing but a skirt and a blouse.'[5] If her wish had been granted, it would have been a strong departure from her style before her illness and would have seen the 'Cinderella of the Pampas' return to her humble roots.

On 4 June 1952, President Perón was sworn in for his second term as president of Argentina. Eva refused to miss the second inauguration ceremony. She wanted to celebrate her husband's success and the triumph of the Peronist party in gaining the support of first-time female voters. Even though she was extremely frail and in so much pain that she could barely stand, she bravely endured her last public appearance. A custom frame of plaster and wire was constructed and attached to the floor of the president's car, which, concealed under Eva's oversize fur coat, allowed the heavily sedated

First Lady to stand shoulder to shoulder with her husband during the celebratory parade through Buenos Aires. Upon her return to the Unzué Palace, Eva took another two doses of pain medication before retiring to her room. Whether she was aware of it at the time, the 4 June would also mark her retirement from the public life that she loved and which gave her existence so much meaning.

Eva's appearance at Perón's inauguration came as a shock for many. Perón himself was dismayed by his wife's suffering:

> Those days were an inferno for Evita. She had become skin alone, through which could be seen the whiteness of her bones. Only her eyes seemed alive and articulate. They moved from person to person and they asked questions of everyone; sometimes they were serene, sometimes they expressed feelings of utter loss.[6]

A mass was even said for the return to health of Eva Perón at London's Brompton Oratory.[7] One of the final photographs taken of her in June, shows a tragic figure far removed from the image of the people's princess dressed in Dior that had permeated the national consciousness. The Eva in the photo is extremely emaciated[8] and the outline of her kneecaps can be seen under the trousers that she wore with a wool jumper, white socks and brogues. By this time, even her iconic chignon had been replaced with plaits which must have been more comfortable.

By the beginning of July, Eva was still being kept in the dark as to the cancer diagnosis that was ravaging her body. The churches were filled with Argentines begging God to preserve her life, not just because it was decreed by the Peronist government, but because Eva Perón was the ultimate symbol of the six-year Peronist regime. They were fearful that without her, the military may destroy Perón, just as they had made him back in 1943, which could result in longer working hours and a cut to living standards. While the country prayed for her recovery, Eva was placated with talk of a trip that she and the president would make together later that year. Knowing how important fashion was his to wife, Juan Perón sent for Paco Jamandreu to try and raise Eva's spirits. The designer arrived at the presidential residence with fabric swatches and sketches in the guise of working with Eva to make her believe that they were creating a new wardrobe. Whether she knew more about her terminal illness than her friends and family believed, or she had suddenly become thrifty, she instead asked Jamandreu to alter several suits that she already owned to fit her shrunken body. Jamandreu would be rewarded for his unwavering loyalty to Eva with a new car.[9]

In 2015, Daniel Nijensohn, a neurosurgeon at Yale University Medical School, published an academic article in *Neurosurgical Focus* stating that he had found evidence that Eva underwent a prefrontal lobotomy in 1952. After discovering signs of drilled holes in radiographs of her skull, his investigation led him to believe that the procedure had been performed on her without her consent by American neurosurgeon, Dr James L. Poppen. As the treatment of illnesses suffered by political leaders and members of the royal family is often kept secret from the public, Nijensohn has theorised that the motive for the operation may not have been as benign as purely trying to treat Eva's cancer-related pain. Numerous accounts survive of President Perón declining to spend time at his wife's sick bed as he 'was bothered by her complaints, by the smell from the secretions, and by everything that had to do with wound care and dressing changes.'[10] Nijensohn believes that Perón was also concerned about how Eva's recent revolutionary behaviour may impact her loyal followers, and the country as a whole. After the failed revolt in 1951, it would appear that from her sickbed, Eva had used her contacts with Prince Bernhard of the Netherlands to purchase weapons and ammunition that she paid for through the Eva Perón Foundation. Eva's heightened anxiety after her surgery brought about a paranoia that Peronism could be under threat.

She planned for the weapons to be used to train workers' militias who would defend her and her cause at all costs. The fact that Eva circumvented Perón's authority to carry out this plan worried the president. While the exact motives for the lobotomy may never be known, Daniel Nijensohn has put forward evidence of a sinister conspiracy theory led by Juan Perón to calm his wife and modify her irrational behaviour. If a lobotomy did take place, the procedure only sped up Eva's decline as she stopped eating soon after.

Eva fell into a coma on the afternoon of 18 July but woke again with a start at midnight. To the shock of family and friends gathered around her bedside, she got up out of bed uttering 'What has happened to me? I have to get out of bed. If I don't, I will die!'[11] Those last lucid days were spent with her mother, siblings, husband, and her confessor Father Benítez. Knowing that death was upon her, Eva wrote her will in which she stated how her love of luxury would continue to support her *descamidados* from beyond the grave: 'My jewellery does not belong to me. Most of it was given to me by my people, but even the pieces I received from friends, from foreign governments or from Perón, must return to the people.' Her last, and most personal wish was for the woman who had ultimately made the biggest impact on her life: 'I ask the General to give, as long as she is alive and God wills it, 3,000 pesos a month to Mama and he should never forget *doña* Juana, whom I am unable to forget.'

María Eva Duarte de Perón passed away in her bedroom at the Unzué Palace on Saturday 26 July 1952. Radio broadcasts and cinema screenings throughout Argentina were interrupted with the public announcement that 'the Press Secretary's Office of the Presidency of the Nation fulfils its very sad duty to inform the people of the Republic that at 20:25 hours, Mrs Eva Perón, Spiritual Leader of the Nation, died.' She was 33 years old. At 10:30pm that evening, the Henriette Fashion House received an urgent call from the presidential residence requesting the presence of head seamstress, and one of Eva's loyal stylists, Asunta Fernández. Upon her arrival,

Juan Perón took her to one side and told her 'Asunta, you have always dressed her, and you will have to dress her now as well.'[12] Fernández worked through the night to transform a white satin Jacques Fath gown into a shroud. The couture dress was one of two dresses that Eva had commissioned Asunta to travel to Europe in February that year to select. Despite her rapidly declining health, Eva had hoped to wear the gowns to the 25 May and 9 July galas. When she died, 'she left no fewer than 150 evening gowns in her wardrobe',[13] including an early Christion Dior *Caprice* evening gown.

Another visitor to the Unzué Palace that night was Spanish pathologist Dr Pedro Ara. Ara was a renowned embalmer and he set to work almost immediately to prepare Eva's body for lying in state. It is unlikely that Eva wished for her blood to be replaced with glycerine to preserve her organs and give the appearance of deep sleep, and it seems more likely that Juan Perón took the decision to immortalise his wife. While Ara undertook his macabre task, Eva's hairdresser Julio Alcaraz styled her hair for the final time. Sara Gatti also completed the task that Eva, conscious of her image to the last, had asked of her. Gatti replaced the bold red Helena Rubenstein nail varnish on Eva's fingers with a transparent Revlon colour that was more suitable for the body of the 'Spiritual Leader of the Nation'.

Preparations for national mourning in Argentina had been planned for some months. Immediately following Eva's death, thirty days of mourning were declared. Businesses closed, the government suspended all official activities, flags were flown at half-mast for ten days on government buildings, and a bill was submitted to congress declaring 26 July to be a National Day of Mourning forevermore. The General Confederation of Labour (CGT) ordered its members to stop work for two days, and to observe mourning dress consisting of a black jacket, the ubiquitous white shirt, and a black tie for a month. The crowds outside the presidential residence grew overnight after Eva's death was announced and it became apparent that the government had underestimated the public's grief. The grand staging of her funeral, where reality and fiction intermingled with public passion, gave rise to the creation of the myth of Eva Perón.

On the morning of the 27 July, Eva's body was moved to the Ministry of Labour to lie in state. The city streets were thronged with crowds who queued for hours in the rain to say a final goodbye to Evita. Her body was displayed in a silk-lined wooden coffin with a glass lid that rendered her face and upper-body visible, draped with the Argentine flag. Many who came broke down at the coffin and had to be led away by nurses from the Eva Perón Foundation. As the third and final day of the lying in state came to a close, it became obvious to officials that thousands of people were still waiting outside the ministry (with lines stretching for over thirty blocks in Buenos Aires) for their opportunity to process past the coffin. The decision was made to extend the ceremony, and for another thirteen days an approximate 2 million mourners viewed the final transformation of their beloved Evita into legend. The outpouring of grief represented the genuine loss that many Argentines felt upon her death. Small candlelit alters dedicated to Eva appeared in neighbourhoods throughout the country, continual Catholic masses were said for her soul, and flower shops ran out of blooms. Even cynics of Peronism in Argentina and abroad saw the nation's collective grief as 'genuine and deep and demonstrated that Evita, who had contributed so strongly to the totalitarianism and bankruptcy of her country, had also won its love'.[14] Messages of condolence poured in from around the world. Among the first cables to be received by Juan Perón was from Queen Elizabeth II (whose mother Eva had so desperately wanted to meet during her Rainbow Tour), that read: 'I extend to you my deepest sympathy and that of my people for the tragic loss which you and the Argentine people have suffered in the premature death of your brilliant and devoted partner.'[15] Eva's notoriety and publicity from the Rainbow Tour meant that her death was frontpage news. *Life Magazine* reported that 'Eva Perón, the most spectacular Cinderella girl of her time, died last week in her early 30s in Argentina's presidential palace.'[16]

On Saturday 9 August, Eva's body was transported to the National Congress Building. Awarded full military honours (usually only conferred on presidents who die in office), her coffin was mounted on a gun carriage and moved to the Congress for another day of public viewing. The next day, a Requiem mass was held before the closed casket made its final journey to the General Confederation of Labour building, in accordance with Eva's wishes, to be temporarily laid to rest in the headquarters of the organisation she had controlled. The sombre spectacle featured thirty-nine *descamisados* pulling the gun carriage carrying Eva's flag-draped coffin to the sound of Chopin's funeral march played by a military band. It took the cortege, including President Perón, Eva's family and members of the cabinet, three hours to pass through the crowded and silent streets of Buenos Aires. Upon reaching the CGT building, Eva's body was given over to Dr Ara to finish the preservation of her remains. There, her body was to remain until a fitting memorial and tomb could be built. Plans were drawn up for a monument that was to be larger than the Statue of Liberty, featuring a representation of a *descamidado*. Eva's body would then be laid to rest in the base of the statue. While the monument was under construction, Eva's body was kept surrounded by flowers and was regularly visited by her mother and sisters. The 1955 *Revolución Libertadora* that ended Juan Perón's second term as president concluded any hope of the monument being finished. Perón fled to Paraguay without making arrangements for the safekeeping of Eva's body.

The new military regime went to great lengths to destroy the legacy of Juan and Eva Perón. Decree Law 4161/56, passed in 1956, banned the mere mention of the couple's names, and the display of any Peronist memorabilia was outlawed. With Juan Perón out of the way, the new regime was naturally afraid that

Eva's body may become a shrine for Peronists and had it removed from the CGT building. Thus began a chapter of Eva's story that would sound completely implausible if it wasn't true. Her body's whereabouts would remain a mystery for sixteen years. First, it was hidden around the country before being stored in a wooden box inside a warehouse at military intelligence headquarters. In 1957, after secret negotiations with Pope Pius XII, 'Operation Europe' was implemented, which resulted in Eva receiving a safe burial in Milan's Musocco Cemetery under the assumed name of Maria Maggi. She remained undisturbed in her Italian grave for fourteen years, until July 1971.

With no body to inspire the devotion of the Peronists, the military regime attempted to erase all memory of the Peróns in Argentina. What the government found that it couldn't destroy was the adoration that many Argentines still felt for Eva. In lieu of a grave in which to pay their respects, Peronists created secret shrines to Evita in their homes and worshipped her portrait. It seemed that no matter how hard the new regime tried to eliminate Evita from the collective hearts and minds of Argentines, her legacy proved to be enduring. Following civil unrest in Argentina, the regime believed that returning the symbolic remains of Eva may help to restore calm and ordered the exhumation of Eva's body. Her corpse was flown to Spain and returned to the care of General Perón and his third wife, Isabel, who kept the body in their Madrid dining room. The body had suffered accidental damage during its transportation around the world and had also been the subject of violence by opponents of Peronism. The nuns of la Merced of Madrid created a new shroud,[17] made from three veils in the colours of the Argentine flag, to cover Eva's body during its time in Spain, and it was blessed in September 1971. This shroud sold at Christie's in 2004 for €160,100.

Eva's body would finally make it back home to Argentina in 1974, when Isabel repatriated her remains to be displayed next to those of her late husband, who had died in office. Plans for a monument to them both was abandoned as political unrest broke out in the country. Juan and Eva would eventually be parted for the final time. Eva's body was given to the Duarte family who quickly, and without ceremony, buried it in the family tomb in La Recoleta Cemetery in Buenos Aires. Successive governments have taken frequently more elaborate measures to secure the tomb and Eva's coffin now rests 6 metres underground in a second compartment of the tomb, undisturbed and finally at peace.

Chapter 9

Legacy

Eva Perón's legacy in Argentina has undergone as many transformations as the woman herself. Eva spent barely six years of her life in the public eye, but the intensity of those years has meant that the name Eva Perón has transcended both time and legend. In the history of South America, only Evita has ever achieved such power and influence, and has therefore been as scrutinised and polarising. She was 'a rabble-rouser in a Dior gown; a vindictive social upstart; God's gift to the Argentine working-classes; President Perón's biggest asset and President Perón's biggest handicap; the subject of dozens of smoking-room jokes – and the cause of millions of passionate prayers.'[1] A central question continues to keep Eva's life in the spotlight. How did a woman from such an impoverished background achieve such unparalleled success in the privileged and machismo society of Argentine politics?

The truth has been difficult for many to accept – María Eva Duarte de Perón was a self-made woman. She was driven by personal ambition to succeed in whatever she set her mind to. The sheer force of her own will led her to leave home as a teenager and move to Buenos Aires to become the actress that she had always dreamed of being. Her love of film magazines and their aspirational stories of fame and fortune taught her to invent her own public image early on, and to accept and use any myths and inconstancies that appeared to her advantage. 'She created a character,' said her hairdresser, Julio Alcaraz. 'In her public life she created a character for herself, and she lived this character totally.'[2] Eva transformed herself into the 'common-people's princess', by appearing on the political stage as the incarnation of an Argentine Cinderella. She empowered the masses and elicited their adoration by showing that even the most disenfranchised could rise to the heady heights of power. She represented a living, breathing success story for the working classes (and a nightmare for the upper classes). Even when she was working as part of Juan Perón's propaganda strategy, her individual political work, that included the creation of her Foundation, allowed her the opportunity to build her own 'brand' of Eva Perón that would be recognisable worldwide via the blonde chignon, tailored suits and glamorous gowns. It could be argued that Eva was one of, if not, the first of First Ladies to outshine their husband on the international stage. Her independent and outspoken nature gave her the strength to be more than just the president's wife, but also attracted criticism from those who believed that she was overstepping her duties as a loyal and humble wife to suit her own agenda and become the most powerful woman of her time.

There is no doubt that the Peróns made a brilliant political team, but even Juan Perón had sometimes been shocked by his wife's emotionally charged rhetoric. 'You are too much of a Peronist,' he told her on occasions. Without her by his side, Perón may have thought himself better placed to deal with the worsening economic crisis that was harming the regime. Instead, without Eva there to protect him, vocal opposition began to grow against him. His decision to attract foreign investment in Argentina was deemed unpatriotic, and his controversial plans to legalise prostitution and divorce was met with condemnation by the Catholic Church. Perón's love life was also dragged into the spotlight when he was accused of being in a relationship with the teenager Nelly Rivas. Events came to a head in June 1955, when Catholic elements in the Argentine Navy and Air Force bombed a Peronist rally in the Plaza de Mayo; ultimately, 364 people were killed in the coup attempt against Perón, with his supporters retaliating by attacking churches throughout Buenos Aires. The damage had been done. A nationalist Catholic alliance from the military, led by Admiral Issac Rojas, General Eduardo Lonardi, and General Pedro E. Aramburu, orchestrated an uprising on 16 September 1955. The junta deposed Perón and established a new provisional government. Fighting broke out across Argentina, and Perón, fearing the outbreak of civil war, resigned the presidency and fled to Paraguay.

The *Revolución Libertadora* junta used Eva's clothing and jewels as evidence of the Peróns' outrageous taste for the finer things in life. Eva's personal belongings, including her extensive wardrobe and jewellery collection, were forcibly taken from the Unzué Palace and inventoried. The military government created investigative commissions to select pieces that would be sold at auction in the process of liquidating assets. Some garments went missing and others were purposely damaged when they were stolen from the presidential residence; Eva's initials were removed from accessories and some of her garments were cut up.[3] In a bid to destroy the Peróns' reputation, the new president, Eduardo Lonardi, ordered a public exhibition of the couple's belongings to be put on display at the Casa Rosada in Buenos Aires. By presenting the objects, believed to be worth more than $6,500,000, as symbols of Peronist excess, the new regime hoped to eradicate all remaining support for Eva and Juan. Over 500 dresses, 600 hats, and 3 rows of dozens of pairs of shoes were displayed across 6 rooms. The number and value appeared shamefully out of touch for the supposed First Lady of the shirtless, and in opposition to Eva's 'fanciful notion that her jewels and dresses could help untold thousands of people for years into the future'.[4] The junta brought on board the press to interpret the luxury horde for the rest of Argentina and South America. The Brazilian illustrated weekly magazine *O Cruzeiro* published an article declaring:

> For more than two months a crowd of Argentines have been squeezed into long lines in the Plaza de Francia to see the

> incredible and fabulous treasure that the Peronist dictatorship could not carry in its hasty flight to Paraguay. Exhibited at the Government House in Buenos Aires, Eva Perón's jewels dazzle viewers... Perón's splurge can be appreciated by the superfluous amount of rare furs, dresses, shoes and jewellery that Evita left behind. Her death occurred almost four years ago and this collection was acquired approximately four years before her death. Hats, dresses and shoes are almost all of an unrefined taste. It seems that the fashion houses of Paris, sent the wife of the Argentine dictator suits that went more with her former role of actress than with that of first lady.[5]

The junta's attempts to discredit Eva led to her legacy becoming conflicted. To her opponents, the exhibition was evidence that Eva was just a demagogic symbol of the hypocritical nature of Peronism. But for her supporters, the display of her dresses and jewels had little impact because Eva had never hidden them. They were the glittering embodiments of their Cinderella princess who they now, in death, viewed as a saint. After the exhibition, many of Eva's dresses and accessories were stored in a bank vault in the Municipal Bank, where they remained until they were restored to the Duarte family after a lengthy court case in the 1990s. This collection of clothing and accessories, totalling approximately 1,500 objects, is on long-term loan to the Museo Evita, a museum dedicated to the memory of Eva Perón that opened on the 50th anniversary of her death in 2002. Founded by Eva's great-niece and housed in a mansion that was once used by the Eva Perón Foundation as a shelter for women and children, the museum is now a popular tourist attraction. The Museo, and the research it has undertaken, has played a large part in dispelling myths and rumours that exist – many perpetuated by a certain musical.... Through the exhibits, the Museo has constructed an image of Eva, using her clothes to embody the brief but intense seven stages of her personal and public life: the ambitious teenager, the actress, the Rainbow of Argentina, the First Lady, the charitable Eva of the Eva Perón Foundation, the politician, and the Eva of *La Razón de mi vida*.

It is rare for so many items of clothing belonging to a controversial historical figure to have survived. That they weren't destroyed after President Perón was overthrown in 1955 is perhaps testament to how much Eva's style and clothing was linked to her as a person. The impact of a particular garment can be powerful, even when removed from the wearer's body. Eva's use of clothing as a means of communication alongside her work has been one of her most enduring legacies. Through her love and knowledge of fashion, Eva appropriated trends such as Christian Dior's New Look, to forge her own distinctive image. She was able to reflect her life's work to help those less fortunate, with her enduring animosity of the upper classes, through her adoption of a modern, elegant and ultimately feminine style. To highlight the importance to Eva of fashion as a metaphor, the Museo Evita have chosen to exhibit her clothing on specially constructed mannequins sculpted by Sergio Lamana, made to her exact measurements and featuring her instantly recognisable chignon hairstyle. Without Eva's body, a Luis D'Agostino suit is just another suit. But when it is displayed on her form, the deeper meaning behind her decision to adopt a working uniform to distinguish her as a woman who meant business becomes clearer.

Today, over half a century after her death, Evita is still a pivotal figure in Argentina's history. With the election of the self-described anarcho-capitalist Javier Milei to the presidency in 2023, the nostalgia for Eva only seems to grow. Her personality, political motives and historical relevance are still debated by historians. In her book, *Eva Perón: The Myths of a Woman*, cultural anthropologist Julie M. Taylor claims that Eva's enduring legacy is due to the combination of three factors: femininity, spiritual power, and revolutionary leadership. Taylor claims that only a woman can ever embody all three factors that allows them to lay a claim to power. She also argues that a fourth factor exists in Eva's ongoing importance in Argentina: the power that her death has over the public imagination.

'Prostitute', the slur most often used against Eva, is not new and continues to be used against women in positions of power to this day. Eva Perón's legacy has been the victim of machismo culture that still wants to judge her against the Catholic ideals and values that permeate Hispanic nations. The fear that her power generated in parts of Argentine society during her lifetime was responsible for much of the malicious gossip about Evita that exists today.

Historian Kelsey Walker has concluded that the change in the image presented of Eva by the media came about because of the 'shift in public opinion regarding women and their legitimacy in positions of political office and in publicly visible spaces'[6] that took place early in the Cold War. While Eva was alive, the rumours surrounding her use of men to advance her career and her suspected illegitimacy had been glossed over. Instead, reporters chose to focus on her glamorous appearance, overlooking the fact that she may have manipulated her image to get ahead, as she was the epitome of the modern woman in the public eye. Portrayals of Eva after her death not only coincided with the overthrow of Peronism (and the end of the Peronist monopoly of the Argentine press), but also with a rise in societal pressures on women to take up traditional gender roles as wives and homemakers. Threats from the Cold War created the ideal nuclear family, and a woman like Eva, who was once feted for her use of designer fashion and her political acumen, was no longer celebrated. Her illegitimacy was emphasised after 1952 as the main motivation for her hatred of the upper classes and her life's mission to gain power to take her revenge on those who had wronged her. Journalists became uncomfortable with Eva's influence and began to depict her as a power-hungry vamp, and it is these images that persist today. The publication in the 1950s of Mary Main's biography *The Woman with the Whip*, and journalist Fleur Cowles' *Bloody Precedent*, reflected and legitimised the negative mythology created by anti-Peronists, even though they lacked sources and contained many factual errors.

One of the most prevalent criticisms of Eva that abounds to this day relates to allegations of fascism and antisemitism that have been levelled against the Peróns. The perception that the Peróns were fascists began with Eva's visit to General Franco during her 1947 Rainbow Tour. After the Second World War, Franco's right-wing dictatorship had left Spain politically isolated and in need of an ally. Argentina's choice to have diplomatic relations with Spain had less to do with shared fascist politics, and more to do with the fact that a third of Argentina's population was of Spanish origin. What can't be excused or ignored, is that President Juan Perón allowed Nazi war criminals to enter Argentina to escape prosecution. Even though no evidence exists to prove that Eva played any part in this shameful practice, she has been maligned by critics as a Nazi. In 1997, Argentine journalist Tomás Eloy Martínez refuted these allegations, declaring that Eva 'was not a fascist – ignorant, perhaps, of what that ideology meant. And she was not greedy. Though she liked jewellery, furs and Dior dresses, she could own as many as she desired without the need to rob others…'[7] Something that contradicts the allegations of antisemitism is Eva's often overlooked work to support the new Jewish state of Israel. Argentina was the first country in Latin America to send food, and the Eva Perón Foundation provided medicine and blankets in large quantities to the Israeli people. Israeli Labour Minister, and future Prime Minister, Golda Meir, met with Eva in April 1951 to personally thank her for the aid that the Foundation had given. The meeting between the Peróns and the Israeli delegation was a public confirmation of the nation's friendships. In many of her speeches, Eva had argued that it was Argentina's oligarchy that upheld antisemitic attitudes, not Peronists. This public support for the Jewish state gave the Argentine government a chance to refute the claims of Nazism made by the opposition, but also generated internal criticism from right-wing nationalists who already opposed Eva's position.

The construction and dissemination of Eva's image worldwide during her lifetime granted her international fame and established her status as an Argentine icon. The power that images of Eva attending official events, or depicting her as a saint, had for her supporters in maintaining her legacy is addressed by Political theorist and historian Gustavo Castagnola:

> These pictures are a powerful symbol of what this leader epitomised for her followers: this is a representation of a young woman who, from her humble origins, had reached the very top of Argentine society; her presence in the most important places of the country wearing dresses designed by the most important houses of Europe concentrated everything women of that time, particularly the humble ones, dreamt of.[8]

Eva's feminine but powerful style has continued to influence fashion throughout the twentieth century. South African-born designers Raemonde and Dora Rahvis took inspiration from famous women for their Rahvis couture spring 1956 collection. Alongside a green 'Grace Kelly' cocktail dress, a pink wool suit with a wide white collar was named 'Eva Perón'. The return of Juan Perón to Argentina in the early 1970s created a resurgence in Peronism. Photographs of Eva began to circulate among younger generations of Argentines showing the former First Lady with her hair loose, and informally dressed in trousers and a shirt. These images were in stark contrast to the formal images that had been admired during Eva's lifetime and reflected Eva's significance to young (often working) women who aspired to make a difference. An example of changing attitudes to Eva occurred in 2010, when the late Argentina fashion designer Jorge Ibáñez presented a collection inspired by Eva, called Evita 2010. Models with recreations of Eva's pompadour hairstyle and blonde chignon walked the catwalk in modern versions of her famous tailored suits and ballgowns. As the collection coincided with Argentina's bicentennial, Ibáñez declared: 'What woman, more than Evita, has represented us during these 200 years?'9

Although there has long been an accepted image of Eva Perón, her ambiguous persona has undergone a significant evolution in the seventy years since her death. Evita's legacy has ricocheted between that of saint and sinner, yet she can be viewed as the perfect example of a popular culture icon because she was ahead of her time. Eva's journey from actress to First Lady was considered scandalous by many during her lifetime, with her detractors accusing her of turning public political life into a showbusiness spectacle. But Eva was creating her own brand of celebrity culture alongside her political role, which saw Argentine citizens – and the wider world – focus on what this glamorous young woman was wearing, saying and doing. The cult of celebrity surrounding Eva has only grown throughout the twentieth and twenty-first centuries, with her rags to riches story appealing to our celebrity-obsessed society.

As early as 1953, the idea of adapting Eva's Cinderella life story for the silver screen was being touted. French actress Andrée Debar, who had been told that she resembled Evita during a film festival in Uruguay, decided to seek the leading rôle in the biopic. She travelled to Buenos Aires in June to meet Juan Perón and seek his approval for the project. 'I explained what we wanted to do,' she said, 'to tell the story of the poor little girl who becomes rich and successful and the wife of the president and wears beautiful clothes and helps the poor.'[10] Perón gave his consent to the film, and Andrée Debar began to garner publicity for her upcoming role. She was featured on the front cover of the 13 June 1953 edition of *Semaine Du Monde,* looking adoringly at a picture of Eva in her lap. Debar was dressed in a strapless blue dress with red corsage at the bust that imitated the famous image of Eva in her Marcel Rochas dress that was featured in *La Razón de mi vida*. Unfortunately for Debar, her dream to portray Eva Perón on film came to nothing.

It would be another twenty-eight years before Faye Dunaway would bring Eva's story to life in the 1981 TV movie *Evita Perón*.

By the late twentieth century, Eva Perón had been the subject of numerous articles, films, books and stage plays. On 21 June 1978, the most successful depiction of Eva's life was presented to a large, and mostly new, audience with the premiere of Andrew Lloyd Webber and Tim Rice's musical *Evita* at the Prince Edward Theatre in London. The idea for a musical adaptation of Eva's life began one evening in 1973 when Tim Rice caught the end of a radio show about Eva. He remembered her face from the Argentine stamps he had collected as a child but was mostly unaware of her historical significance. Rice began researching Eva and even travelled to Buenos Aires to view original documents and meet people who had known her. His fascination with Eva Perón not only led to him collaborating with Andrew Lloyd Webber on the 1976 *Evita* concept album, but also to him naming his first daughter Eva. In their 1996 book, *Evita: The Real Life of Eva Perón*, Nicholas Fraser and Marysa Navarro claimed that the musical's anti-Peronist narrative was based on Mary Main's highly critical 1952 biography of Evita, *The Woman with the Whip*, which Tim Rice has stated (in his view) is the definitive biography. Historical inaccuracies, such as Juana Ibarguren and her children being blocked from Juan Duarte's funeral, or the teenage Eva leaving for Buenos Aires as the mistress of Agustín Magaldi, may have made for a thrilling narrative, but have only added to the myths surrounding Evita. Navarro and Fraser summed up the musical in their biography:

> Although [*Evita*] was based for the most part on the earliest and seamiest versions of Evita's life, something happened to the tale in its retelling and the Evita who emerged each evening, dressed first as a teenager, then a hooker, and finally, in tulle and silver foil, as First Lady, was far from being unsympathetic.[11]

The West End production of Evita closed in February 1986, after 3,176 performances and a Laurence Oliver Award for Best Musical. It also became the first British musical to be awarded the Tony Award for Best Musical for the Broadway production in 1979.

Director Alan Parker's 1996 film adaptation of the musical helped to cement Eva Perón's status as a truly international pop-culture icon. The casting of Madonna, who at the time was one of the biggest, and most controversial, pop stars in the world, was a coup for the producers. The singer had been desperate for the part, later telling reporters: 'This is the role I was born to play. I put everything of me into this because it was much more than a role in a movie. It was exhilarating and intimidating at the same time. And I am prouder of *Evita* than anything else I have done.'[12] She threw herself into research for the role and was rewarded with a Best Actress Golden Globe award for her performance. The production of the film was met with protests in Argentina by those who feared the film would damage Eva's image. Members of the Peronist Party condemned the casting of the overtly sexual Madonna to portray the 'Spiritual Leader of the Nation'. In an attempt to correct some of the more misleading claims perpetuated in the musical, the Argentinean film biography, *Eva Perón: The True Story*, was released in October 1996, starring Esther Gorris in the title role. The film was Argentina's official Academy Award submission for 'Best Foreign Language Film' Academy Award that year.

As with Eva herself, one of the most popular outputs from the film was its impact on fashion designers and trends in the late 1990s. Costume designer Penny Rose was nominated for the BAFTA Award for Best Costume Design for her work on *Evita*. She had travelled to Argentina to look at surviving examples of Eva's clothing and shoes on which she then based her costume designs. Rose collaborated closely with fashion house Salvatore Ferragamo, who had made Eva Perón's shoes during her time as First Lady, and the brand created fourteen pairs of shoes for the film, including exact reproductions of shoes made exclusively for Eva and others in the style of the period.[13] Penny Rose broke the Guinness World Record for 'Most Costume Changes in a Film' for the eighty-five costume changes that Madonna undertook to represent Evita's style progression throughout the film. When interviewed, Rose described Evita as 'the Imelda Marcos of the clothing world … She liked bright colours, big prints and a lot of jewellery.'[14] Working alongside chief cutter Annie Hadley, Rose chose to avoid turning Madonna into a caricature of Eva by using 'a mixture of things that suited Madonna and were in the flavour of Eva'.[15] Overall, the production used more than 5,500 period costumes, many sourced from costume houses around the globe.

Carrying on the tradition of cinema tie-ins that have been around since the Golden Age of Hollywood, numerous fashion brands retailed Evita-inspired garments and accessories. Designers worn by Eva even got in on the act. In Hong Kong, Ferragamo sold limited edition black and red suede 'Evita' heeled sandals based on a design worn by Madonna in the film, priced at HK$5,000. Exhibitions of the replica shoes made for the film toured the world before being added to the collection of the Museo Salvatore Ferragamo in Florence. Nicole Miller sold handbags, Elie Tahari created 1940s-silhouette suits, milliner Deborah Rhodes promoted hats, and Estée Lauder even introduced a makeup line called The Face of Evita.

In a case of pure coincidence, two weeks before the premiere of *Evita*, three of Eva's Christian Dior evening dresses arrived in New York from Buenos Aires to go on display as part of the Metropolitan Museum of Art Costume Institute's Christian Dior exhibition. The curator, Richard Martin, proclaimed the importance of Eva's clothing by telling the *New York Times* that even if the film wasn't being released, the Dior designs 'still would be pieces we would want in the exhibition'.[16] Getting the garments to America was the result of months of intense negotiations between the Duarte family and the Argentine government, leading to the ensembles arriving at the Metropolitan Museum with only twenty-four hours to spare before they were to go on display. The garments loaned from the family and the Argentine Minister of Culture included a strapless pale green silk tulle gown, an embroidered pale pink satin evening coat, and a dark blue silk velvet dress with sequin and bead embroidery, that joined more than eighty other Dior garments in the designer's retrospective.

The memory of Eva in the public consciousness has been raised in the last two decades through a resurgence of items related to the Peróns being sold at auction. In 2011, Mario Rotundo, a former aide to Juan Perón, made headlines when a court blocked his attempts to sell his collection of 14,000 items that had once belonged to the president and Eva. Rotundo claimed that Perón's widow Isabel bequeathed the former president's belongings to him to help fund the social work of his Foundation for Peace and Friendship between Nations. The government-funded Juan Perón Institute raised concerns about the objects being dispersed at auction, asserting that the collection should be turned over to the state as an important part of Argentina's heritage. After the sale was frozen, Mario Rotundo agreed to the Institute's request but publicly stated that the government would have to pay for the possessions. Viewing himself as Juan Perón's heir, Rotundo started civil and criminal proceedings against the Banco Cuidad of Buenos Aires in 2015. He held the bank responsible for losing 95 per cent of Perón's possessions which had been entrusted to their custody after being confiscated by the *Revolución Libertadora* in 1955. Rotundo's use of his 'inheritance' ostracised him from many Peronists, and by his death in 2019 he had been no closer to solving the issues surrounding his claim on Juan and Eva's legacy.

Another auction of Perón memorabilia took place as recently as 2022. A few months after Eva's death, President Perón gifted Paco Jamandreu five of Eva's dresses with a note stating: 'These dresses are yours. Use them for good'. Of the five dresses, four had been designed by Jamandreu and the other was the Jacques Fath design worn by Eva in Numa Ayrinhac's joint portrait of the Peróns. Jamandreu made money by exhibiting the dresses in catwalk shows, constantly altering the garments to fit his models. Upon his death in 1994, the dresses passed into the care of his right-hand woman, Beatriz Gandola, who continued displaying the gowns to honour Jamandreu's legacy. Gandola eventually sold the garments, and they were brought to the auction house of José María Roldán in 2022. Reflecting on Eva Perón's popularity more than half a century after her death, and the historical importance of the couture she owned, the Fath gown was estimated to sell for between 40,000–45,000 dollars.

Eva Perón's transformation into a popular culture icon could be viewed as the final step in her Cinderella metamorphosis. From the little girl poring over photographs of her favourite actresses, her image now looms large over Buenos Aires in the form of two steel images of her that adorn the former Ministry of Public Works. No other First Lady has captured the public's consciousness in the way that Eva has. First Lady Jacqueline Kennedy Onassis may have received the same amount of publicity (if not more) as Eva throughout her life in the public eye, but she came from wealth, did not need to fashion a new image and persona to meet her president, and chose to take a supporting role to her husband's administration. This is possibly why Eva still courts so much aspirational affection, reflected in her enduring fame. The story of her life (and the image she fostered) continues to be of interest, with new productions of *Evita* being mounted on the stage, and even drag queen Roxxxy Andrews choosing to portray Eva in the HERstory of the World musical segment of season two of *RuPaul's Drag Race All Stars*.

Eva Perón's survival as an international figure has its roots in the world of entertainment where Eva first started her meteoric ascent. The spectacles of the musical and film productions of Evita have ultimately created a theatrical version of Eva's life. In publicity for Evita, Alan Parker summarised why he believed the story of Eva Perón has endured:

> While *Evita* is a story of people whose lives were in politics, it is not a political story. It is a Cinderella story about the astonishing life of a girl from the most mundane of backgrounds, who became the most powerful woman her country (and indeed Latin America) had ever seen, a woman never content to be a mere ornament at the side of her husband, the president.[17]

It cannot be denied that Eva Perón remains Argentina's most enduring cultural icon. During all the upheavals that Argentina has faced since her death, Eva has remained safe in the realm of a legend. One quality of Eva's legacy, which both her detractors and supporters seem to agree upon, is that she was an immensely ambitious woman who had a unique affinity with the Argentine masses. Her impact on the popular consciousness forever changed the destiny for many women and resulted in a reframing of women's roles in the Argentine and Latin American social and political spectrum. These women have continued Eva's social work into the twenty-first century.

Chapter 10

Political Copycats

One of Eva Perón's most enduring legacies has been her impact on women in South American politics. Her advocation for women's political rights during the struggle for female suffrage in Argentina also led to a change in the law allowing women to stand for, and be elected to, governmental office. Many Latin American women therefore viewed Eva as bringing about positive changes for her fellow women. In the twenty-first century, Eva's image is still politicised, and her face is currently the symbol of the unemployed Evita Movement, founded in 2004 to bring about social change in Argentina. A number of international First Ladies and female politicians have since taken inspiration from Eva's political style and her image. Even Lisa Simpson has embodied the image of Eva in an episode of *The Simpsons* where she runs for student body president![1] Through their use of powerful oratory, dedication to a particular cause, or by dyeing their hair blonde, Eva continues to be imitated by women in politics to this day.

Women's participation in politics has changed hugely in South America, a region known for its machismo. The influential non-elected role of First Lady has also changed since Eva Perón was in office. The presidential system in both South America and the USA means that the partner of the president plays a visible and powerful part in the country's leadership by supporting their spouse's career, but recent First Ladies have bristled at sacrificing their careers to take on an unelected role. Eva claimed that her life as First Lady was 'dedicated … to conveying to the president the hopes of the people',[2] yet she changed the function of the role beyond all recognition. Juan Perón's dictatorial government afforded Eva the opportunity to redefine the role of First Lady. While undertaking her duties as a political spouse, she also worked within the Ministries of Labour and Health and used the Eva Perón Foundation to improve social welfare in the country. She also set the bar for power dressing for female politicians and First Ladies that have followed.

The undemocratic and anti-feminist aspects of the office of First Lady have often diminished the importance of the role, but with many wives now having their own professional careers and feminist views, the traditional role of First Lady has continued to adapt in South America. In Brazil, First Lady Janja Lula da Silva imitated Eva's approach by reshaping the traditional role. Determined not to be 'the wife who hosts charity teas and visits philanthropic institutions',[3] Lula da Silva has used her profile to talk about public policy and to make solo visits to support causes that are important to her, including empowering women. In stark contrast, former Chilean First Lady, Irina Karamanos, effectively ended the office of First Lady for any future presidential partner in Chile. She felt uncomfortable with the amount of unelected power afforded to her, especially in a country that had only recently emerged from under a military dictatorship. An influential political figure herself, Karamanos chose to transfer the foundations overseen by the First Lady and to close the office. Her reforms were met with support and criticism from feminist groups in Chile, with Karamanos stating:

> I decided that feminist action was more important than feminist image because a lot of criticism came along – that I as a feminist shouldn't be entering the most conservative place in government … But I was like, look, if you want to actually change something, you have to do it from the inside.[4]

Less than a year after Eva's death, Chile elected its first female senator, Maria de la Cruz (1912–1995). de la Cruz was a journalist and writer who, like Eva, had hosted her own radio programme which she used to call for Chilean women's participation in politics. In 1946 she founded the Feminine Party of Chile, whose membership of working- and middle-class women were ultimately successful in bringing about a change in the law, in 1949, to grant women the right to vote in all elections. de la Cruz came to the attention of General Carlos Ibáñez del Campo, who was impressed by her powerful speeches and her skills as a campaigner. He hired her as his presidential campaign manager for the 1952 election. de la Cruz swung into action to entice female voters to Ibáñez, who, as 'a friend of Argentina's Perón, campaigned on Perón-like themes with Maria de la Cruz, head of the Partido Feminino, who even resembles the late Evita'.[5] Ibáñez was duly elected and *Life Magazine* commented on de la Cruz's abilities by stating: 'The women of Chile voted for a president … The petticoated politicos quickly got behind Carlos Ibáñez, the onetime dictator-president who was thrown out in 1931 by the menfolk.'[6] Maria de la Cruz was sworn in as a senator in February 1953, but her political career was short lived. Just like Eva Perón, she faced opposition from those who were suspicious of her rise to power, resulting in politically motivated accusations of smuggling. After being removed from Congress, Maria was never again able to regain her former influence. Even though women had made some ground in politics, some spheres of 1950s South America were still hostile to women holding governmental positions.

Juan Perón's third wife, Isabel,[7] was, in a cruel twist of fate, able to live out Evita's unrealised dream of running Argentina. She succeeded where Eva had failed by being chosen as Perón's vice presidential running mate when the couple took office upon Perón's return from exile in 1973. She held this office concurrently with that of First Lady, and ultimately became the world's first woman to serve as president of a country upon the death of her husband in July 1974. Her short and controversial regime was plagued by labour unrest, inflation and violence. With allegations of embezzlement of public funds, murders, disappearances and the erosion of constitutional rights, Argentina was on the brink of anarchy by 1976. Isabel Perón was eventually arrested and deposed by the military on 24 March 1976, and, after serving five years under house arrest, would go into exile in Spain in 1981. Would Eva Perón's life have played out similarly to Isabel's if she had lived? Eva and Isabel's shared love for the same man and their bleached hair drew external comparisons, but Isabel was ideologically more right-wing in her political beliefs than Eva, and she lacked the charisma and speech-making skills that made Evita so popular. The secret support that existed for Eva after Perón was overthrown in 1955 is telling in that the same was never afforded to Isabel after she was deposed.

Eva Perón's political successor in Argentina appeared in the form of Cristina Fernández de Kirchner. Born less than a year after Eva's death, Fernández grew up in a single-mother household like Eva. She came of age during a heated time in Argentine politics that saw the decline of the military government of the Argentine Revolution, the return of Juan Perón as president, and the beginning of The Dirty War that saw between 22,000 and 30,000 people murdered or vanish without a trace. While studying law at the University of La Plata, she met her future husband, Néstor Kirchner, who was a member of Peronist student groups. Following Néstor into politics, as a member of Juan and Eva Perón's Justicialist Party, Cristina served as a senator in both legislative houses, an office that she continued to hold during her husband's presidency from 2003–2007. The parallels between Eva and Cristina are obvious, and Fernández has not shied away from exploiting them. Both women began their political apprenticeships as ambitious and enthusiastic First Ladies who rose in status alongside their husbands, while winning the support of the poor through generous public spending. Cristina's image also transformed as she became a powerful force within the Peronist movement. Gone were the smart, sober suits from her time as a young senator, and in their place were designer clothes, accessories and ostentatious jewellery.

Reports noted that on foreign trips Cristina took a lesson from Eva's book by travelling with trunks of clothes so that she could change her outfit regularly.

When Néstor Kirchner decided not to run for a second term in 2007 in favour of his wife, Cristina's glamorous appearance became a major point of debate. With the two main candidates for president being women, the election inevitably focused on appearance. Cristina's critics pointed out that the 54-year-old presidential hopeful suddenly had a fresher and tighter face, leading to speculation that she had gone 'under the knife'. In such an aesthetic-obsessed era, Cristina's heavy make-up and alleged cosmetic surgery were used against her, in that they created an inappropriate image for a head of state. Elisa Carrió, Fernández's main rival during the election, dismissed the idea that Cristina's makeover was an attempt to capture the magic of Eva Perón. 'Eva was a political heroine, a real queen, not a Botox queen,'[8] Carrió bluntly said. Fernández's supporters jumped to her defence by highlighting that her overt femininity hadn't impacted on her successful career as a lawyer and senator, and that women of any age had the right to look glamorous. Fernández herself asked interviewers a question that Eva had been asked multiple times during her political career, 'Would I have to dress like I was poor in order to be a good political leader?'[9]

Cristina Fernandez de Kirchner was elected president in 2007, making her the first elected female president in Argentine history. 'The New Evita' proclaimed her desire to be her own woman, 'I don't want to inherit anything from Eva, or from [my husband] Kirchner. Everything I've got is a result of my own achievements, and my own defects too.'[10] Just as Juan Perón lost his spouse at an important moment in his presidency, so too did Cristina. Néstor Kirchner died suddenly of a heart attack in 2010. Instrumental in Cristina's ascent to power was the spousal devotion she showed to Néstor, even after his passing. In the same way that Eva had made her role as Perón's wife central to her image, Cristina was able to embody this conservative outlook to prove her superiority over her female opponents. She underwent a second metamorphosis into the grieving black-clad widow. Her use of mourning as a political tool garnered her new support from sympathetic Argentines who re-elected her for a second four-year term in 2011.

Fernández's presidency saw a return to Peronist iconography. When questioned on her views on feminism she answered in a very similar way to how Eva described herself in *La Razón de mi vida*, by declaring that she was a 'Peronist, not a feminist.'[11] She paid tribute to Evita in 2012 by unveiling a new 100 peso note featuring an image of the former First Lady to commemorate the 60th anniversary of Eva's death. Fernández said at the time, 'It's not that Eva was a saint. It's not that she didn't make mistakes … She was a humble woman of the people. Honouring her with this bill is a way of recovering justice.'[12] As Cristina's eight years in office were dogged by allegations of corruption, it is compelling that she may have been drawing comparisons between herself and Evita by referring to Eva's 'mistakes'.

When Fernández's term of office came to an end in 2015, the Justicialist Party spent four years in opposition before Alberto Fernández was miraculously elected president, with Cristina as his vice president. Even with eleven corruption cases opened against her, Cristina presented herself as a champion of the people, invoking the cult of Eva Perón to cling onto power. Her grip on power finally gave out when she was convicted of corruption in 2022, sentenced to six years in prison, and banned from ever holding public office again. Not since Eva was First Lady of Argentina had a woman held so much concentrated power for so long as Cristina Fernández de Kirchner. For both women, politics was an intensely personal journey, shaped by their supporters and those who vehemently opposed them. Cristina was ultimately able to surpass Eva's political power (that was quashed by conservative opponents in the government, and by her untimely death) by succeeding her husband to the presidency, which she was able to hold with a solid majority. However, her now tattered political career and reputation may never be able to match those of Evita's.

Another female politician who has drawn comparisons to Eva Perón is the Democrat US Representative for New York's 14th congressional district, Alexandria Ocasio-Cortez (AOC). Born to a working-class Puerto Rican family in the Bronx, New York, Ocasio-Cortez has had a meteoric rise to the centre of American politics. Taking office at 29, she became the youngest woman ever to serve in the US Congress. With over 8 million followers on Instagram, and her advocacy for progressive causes such as Medicare for All, a Green New Deal, and free college tuition, Ocasio-Cortez is a vocal opponent of the Republican Party and Donald Trump. Much like the vitriol that Eva faced, Ocasio-Cortez's background, youth, gender, image and socialist policies have all made her a prime target for criticism from members of the Republican Party. While Eva's career as a mediocre actress was mocked by her rivals, President Trump has disparagingly referred to the Green New Deal as the work of 'a young bartender', in a reference to Ocasio-Cortez's work before entering politics. The support she has gained as a politician has also been ridiculed. In a 2019 campaign video, Republican candidate Michelle Nix belittled Ocasio-Cortez by stating: 'She has the media. She has the followers. But bless her heart, she has some terrible ideas.'[13]

AOC was first compared to Eva Perón in a 2018 article on the right-wing website The Stream, where she was called 'The Democrats' New Evita Perón.'[14] Her elevation in the Democratic Party resulted in the media taking note, and it was in the aftermath of AOC covering the April 2019 edition of *Time* magazine that conservative commentator Charlie Sykes remarked to *The Guardian*: 'She looks like Evita. She's obviously an exciting and charismatic figure, but I'm not sure she represents the direction that Democrats want to take in 2020.'[15]

President Trump's views on one of his fiercest critics were published in Tim Alberta's 2019 book, *American Carnage: On the Front Lines of the Republican Civil War*. Trump stated that he first saw Ocasio-Cortez during her primary to become Congresswoman, 'I see a young woman, ranting and raving like a lunatic on a street corner … I said, "That's Eva Perón. That's Evita."'[16] Unwittingly referring to Andrew Lloyd Webber and Tim Rice's song, *The Lady's Got Potential* from *Evita*, Trump told Alberta: 'She's got talent. Now, that's the good news. The bad news: she doesn't know anything. She's got a good sense, an "it" factor, which is pretty good, but she knows nothing. But with time, she has real potential.'[17] Ocasio-Cortez welcomed the comparison with a thread of tweets attributing quotes to 'Evita Perón' including: 'I know that, like every woman of the people, I have more strength than I appear to have.'[18] Trump may have been being generous in his comparison of AOC with Eva, as his political career also shared many similarities with that of Evita. Trump, who had previously admitted in his 2004 book, *Trump: Think Like a Billionaire: Everything You Need to Know About Success, Real Estate, and Life*, that his favourite Broadway show was *Evita*, may have seen himself as a modern 'Spiritual Leader of the Nation'. His evolution from reality TV star to president of the United States mirrored that of Eva's rise from actress to First Lady. In an interview with ABC News, Syracuse University associate professor of music history, Amanda Eubanks Winkler, also drew parallels between Perón's appeal to the '*Descamisados*', and Trump's 2016 campaign that reached 'out to people, working-class people and you can see that in terms of the demographics of folks who voted for him'.[19]

Just like Eva, Ocasio-Cortez enjoys fashion and has faced criticism from Republicans who have deemed her hypocritical for wearing designer clothing while campaigning for socialist causes. As with Eva's choice to dress in Dior, Ocasio-Cortez's decision to wear high-end clothing (often rented or borrowed) does not seemed to have impacted on her popularity and may even have attracted her new supporters as she was named one of fashion search engine Lyst's Power Dressers of 2020.[20] Ocasio-Cortez has also not shied away from making political statements with her fashion choices. At her 2019 swearing-in ceremony, she chose to wear a white trouser suit (white having been used as a symbol of political resistance by the suffragettes), with gold hoop earrings that reflected her heritage. She later tweeted: 'Next time someone tells Bronx girls to take off their hoops, they can just say they're dressing like a Congresswoman.'[21] Her most famous use of fashion to send a message was during her first appearance at the Met Gala in 2019. Dressed in a strapless white gown with a tulle mermaid skirt, designed by Aurora James for Brother Vellies, the gown was emblazoned with bold red embroidered letters proclaiming, 'Tax the rich.' Ocasio-Cortez hit back at her critics by stating that 'The medium is the message,'[22] and that her dress was borrowed. Just as Eva became known for her iconic chignon hairstyle, AOC regularly appears wearing Stila Cosmetics red lipstick in homage to her Latina heritage. She has spoken about the importance of femininity and beauty and how these things are often used misogynistically against women in politics.

Eva's influence has also permeated to politicians born after the Millenium. Ofelia Fernández (born 2000) became the youngest lawmaker in Latin America when she was elected to the Buenos Aires City Legislature in 2019. Aged only 19, Fernández had stood as a candidate for the Peronist Frente de Todos coalition. The activist and feminist had been a strong supporter for the legalisation of abortion in Argentina and she assumed her seat as a Buenos Aires legislator wearing a striking red dress and bleached blonde hair. Her adoption of Eva's trademark hair colour was notable to many commentators who proclaimed Ofelia as the face of the new generation in Argentine politics. Unlike Eva, Ofelia has had to navigate the political landscape alongside social media. She has been honest about the misogynistic abuse and the attacks on her physical appearance that have been directed at her online, 'They try to force you out of the political conversation by concentrating on your looks, your wages, your clothes. There are hardly any moments in which hostility is aimed against a solid idea or something I said: It's not an ideological conflict – it's just obvious violence.' Even though seventy years have passed since Eva's death, it is sad that physical appearance is still used as the basis to judge and attack women in leadership roles.

The twentieth and twenty-first centuries have seen multiple women step up to fill the political void left by Eva Perón. A transformation in Argentine society has led to a re-examination of Eva's legacy, which now credits her passion and activism for bringing about a desire for social justice and equal rights that later generations have taken on board. It was also the result of Eva's Peronist campaigning that women in Argentina have been able to occupy the public space she created. Historian and journalist, Araceli Bellota, has credited Eva for making 'it possible for a woman whose parents were workers, like Cristina [Fernández de Kirchner], to attend a university and prepare for a career. And that's what enabled her to be president.'[23]

Epilogue

No woman has ever possessed so much power in the political life of a country as Eva Perón…[1]

Over seventy years have passed since the untimely death of Eva Perón, yet her status as a popular culture and feminist icon has not diminished. Eva's life at the heart of Argentine politics as First Lady spanned just six years, during which she was both feted and vilified as one of the most glamourous women of her generation. Yet the intensity of her time in the public eye has embedded her into the collective consciousness of Argentines. Her life is still appealing to our celebrity-obsessed age because her story ultimately confirms one of Hollywood's oldest cliches, the rags to riches story. The former Minister of Tourism for the Argentine Republic, Carlos Enrique Meyer, once said: 'No other historical or cultural icon captures the attention of Argentines and visitors alike in quite the same way Evita does. She continues to be our ambassador to travellers from around the world who visit Argentina and want to learn more about our history and culture.'

Her ascent was even more remarkable for the challenges she presented to the conservative society in Argentina, where women did not play a vocal and visible part in public life. She defied the views of women and refused to be seen as an accessory to her husband. Eva's unique role in government and her confident use of propaganda techniques made her an international figure who was often a subject of speculation. While defenders still argue to this day that Peronism supported the most vulnerable in society, the political power wielded by Eva was heavily criticised both inside and outside of Argentina. In a period that reinforced traditional gender roles, that fact that Eva's images monopolised the press next to her husband led to the international press nicknaming her 'The Dictator President'. To her supporters, she was '*la dama de la esperanza*', the lady of hope, who made a real difference to people's lives through her charitable Foundation, and helped women achieve the right to vote. But to her opponents, she would always be an upstart who had forced herself on Juan Perón to take over the country for her own gains. In twenty-first century Argentina, Eva's name is still controversial. To some, she is a symbol of populist hypocrisy, who exploited Argentina's working class to secure political power for herself and her dictator husband. As of 2024, after the election of President Javier Milei, the Peronist party is the largest opposition movement in Argentina. Milei's decision to revoke laws to limit the powers of the trade unions has brought Eva to the forefront as a torchbearer for social justice. For poorer Argentines, the current polarising government has created a wave of nostalgia which has seen Eva's memory transcend politics. Rita Cantero, an elderly woman whose mother was directly supported by Eva, still views the First Lady as an example to look up to. 'For us she is like a saint,' Cantero said. 'Many judged her because she was a woman, but she was an honest, hard-working girl. She fought for our nation and was the force of Perón.'[2]

Although fashion can't be used as a foolproof political barometer, how our leaders use fashion to forward their career is an important decision that is ultimately scrutinised by the electorate. As a political wife, Eva made use of her role as unofficial ambassador for several Argentine and European fashion designers from the 1940s until her death, who helped to create the three strong personas she adopted throughout her life – as an actress, emerging First Lady, and then after her return from the 1947 Rainbow Tour, as a serious political candidate and social reformer. Having a mother who was a seamstress seems to be a prerequisite in rags to riches stories, and

Eva's mother definitely helped to create her daughter's first style through her handmade clothes.

The evolution of her image reflected the transformations that took place in her life and didn't happen by chance. Eva used her knowledge of clothes and glamour (gleaned from film magazines and the cinema) to form her style, with the major turning point in her appearance taking place after her Rainbow Tour. Even though fashion can be accused as being trivial, Eva's clothing demonstrated the close relationship between aesthetics and her politics. Carl Sferrazza Anthony wrote that 'While it can unquestionably create bias, the visual immediacy of the clothes we wear inevitably offers others a glimpse, authentically or not, into who we are at any given moment. Or at least, who we hope to appear to be.'[3] In Eva's case, she created an unspoken dialogue through her image that portrayed the wealth of Argentina to the world, while also representing a romanticised Cinderella come to life for the poor. Even though the upper classes pointed out this hypocrisy, her supporters saw only a passionate woman to whom they could aspire. Before the rise of fashion-conscious First Ladies, including Jacqueline Kennedy and Imelda Marcos, Eva Perón may have been one of the first political wives to be viewed, and judged, as a celebrity.

In *Power Dressing: First Ladies, Women Politicians & Fashion*, fashion journalist Robb Young states:

> Be they mothers of the nation or divisive icons, revolutionary heroines or disgraced populists, globetrotting power brokers or imprisoned dissidents, political women are fascinating characters, handling an intoxicating brew of power and fame, and cultivating personal styles in the full glare of the public eye.[4]

Arguably Eva's most celebrated contribution to fashion was her adoption of the tailored suit, creating a style of workwear worn by women ever since. Through her clothes Eva Perón created the recognisable brand of 'Evita' for her loyal *descamisados*: 'When I chose to be "Evita" I knew I was choosing the path of my people. Now, after making that choice, it is easy for me to show that this was the case. Only the people call me "Evita". Only the *descamisados* learnt to call me that.'[5] The attention focused on her image and style isn't exactly difficult to understand. Just as the fashion choices of Diana, Princess of Wales, are still analysed today, Eva's untimely death has also mythologised her image. Fashion designer Bill Blass once said that Eva's enduring fame, resulting from her rise from nothing and her young death, was an 'unbeatable combination'.

The life of Eva Perón was much more than that portrayed in the musical. She helped to gain the right to vote for Argentine women, founded The Eva Perón Foundation to provide scholarships, homes and hospitals. As with the ongoing press fascination with the clothes (and associated costs to the taxpayer) worn by Catherine, Princess of Wales, it does seem that – despite the progress being made in the spheres of equality and women's rights – not much has changed, and that the male-dominated media still resent powerful women. Eva was aware of this and played the media at their own game, famously posing for Gisèle Freund's camera in front of her bursting wardrobes. The text that accompanies this image, by *Life Magazine*'s correspondent Robert Neville, is forced to highlight Eva's sharpness, in comparison to the age-old presumption that a young blonde woman with an interest in fashion must therefore be an airhead: 'Far from being a rattle-brained blonde, Evita soon showed herself to be a serious-minded young woman with keen political sense and purpose.'[6]

Eva Perón's rise to power could almost be the plot for one of the films she adored as a child – a Cinderella story with a Latin American twist. Through the cult of her personality and her iconic image, Eva was able to enter the memory of Argentina and the wider world in just seven years. Both in condemnation and devotion, Evita's story has transcended time. But when all is said and done, Eva Perón was able to succeed in her wish for immortality. 'I confess that I have an ambition, one single, great personal ambition,' she wrote. 'I would like the name of "Evita" to figure somewhere in the history of my country'.[7]

Acknowledgements

The process of writing is a solitary, and often lonely undertaking, but the task of a getting a book from the idea stage to publication takes a group effort. The acknowledgements page is a chance for me to thank those who have played their part, both large and small, in the creation of this book.

First, I am indebted to Pen & Sword Commissioning Editor Amy Jordan for taking a chance on me and Evita. Years of research have gone into this book, and I am so excited to send it out into the world. I will forever remember the pure joy on opening Amy's email offering me a contract, while standing on the platform at Bristol Temple Meads Station!

I cannot thank Florencia Croizet at the Museo Evita enough for sharing her invaluable knowledge on Eva Perón, and for organising and conducting me on a tour of the museum. What I saw and learnt during that tour opened my eyes to Eva's origins. When the Covid-19 pandemic hit upon my return from Argentina, Florencia kindly continued to assist me even as the world closed around us. I will be forever grateful to her and the Museo Evita for their support. I was greatly aided in my research trip by the Southern Counties Costume Society Research Bursary.

My sincere thanks must go to Piero Cavalletti from Fernanda Gattinoni, Igor Uria, the Collections Director at the Cristóbal Balenciaga Museum, Acacia Echazarreta of the Fundación Museo de la Moda, and Ludovica Barabino of the Fondazione Ferragamo, for their generosity in answering my research queries. All were kind enough to provide me with resources and information relating to Eva's clothes.

The National Archives and Sarah Mitchell, Julie Crocker and Karen Lawson from the Royal Archives were also extremely helpful in providing me with advice and archival documents relating to the British government's view on the Argentine First Lady and Eva's Rainbow Tour. My gracious thanks for the permission of His Majesty King Charles III in allowing me to make use of material from the Royal Archives.

I have been blown away by the support from my friends, family and colleagues. A special shout-out must go to Lucinda Comport, Sarah Cox, Charlotte Eddington, Natalie Fey, Jenny Jones, Keith Lodwick, Abigail Mann, Sabrina Shahid, Sarah Trubshawe, Shelley Tobin, and the committee of the Dress and Textile Specialists for their friendship and for listening to me chatter on about Evita for these past years! To my parents, thank you for being there for me during this process and for never wavering in your belief that I had a book within me.

Bibliography

Books

Anthony, Carl Sferrazza, *Why They Wore It: The Politics & Pop Culture of First Ladies' Fashion*, The Richard Nixon Foundation, 2018.

Aringoli, Guillermo Enrique D'Arino, *Evita en Europa: Un viaje iniciático. La construcción del mito*, Caligrama, 2018.

Barnes, John, *Eva Perón*, W.H. Allen & Co. Ltd, 1978.

Balmaceda, Daniel, *Qué tenían puesto: La moda en la historia argentina*, Sudamericana, 2018.

Benaim, Laurence, *Women in Dior: Portraits of Elegance*, Rizzoli International Publications Inc., 2016.

Benjamin, Walter, *The Work of Art in the Age of Mechanical Reproduction*, Penguin, 2008.

Camarasa, Jorge, *La Enviada. El viaje de Eva Perón a Europa*, Planeta, 1998.

Carlson, Marifran, ¡Feminismo!: The Woman's Movement in Argentina from its Beginnings to Eva Perón, Chicago Review Press, 2005.

Cosgrove, Charles H.; Yeo, Khiok-Khng; Weiss, Herold B., *Cross-Cultural Paul: Journeys to Others, Journeys to Ourselves*, W.B. Eerdmans Publishing Company, 2005.

Cowles, Fleur, *Bloody Precedent: The Peron Story*, Frederick Muller Ltd, 1952.

Ferragamo, Salvatore, *Shoemaker of Dreams: The Autobiography of Salvatore Ferragamo*, George G. Harrap & Co. Ltd.,1957.

Fontaine, Joan, *No Bed of Roses*, William Morrow and Company, 1978.

Foss, Clive, *Juan and Eva Perón*, Sutton Publishing Ltd., 2006.

Fraser, Nicholas and Navarro, Marysa, *Evita: The Real Lives of Eva Perón*, Carlton Publishing Group, 2003.

Gnoli, Sofia, Fernanda Gattinoni, *Moda e stelle ai tempi della Hollywood sul Tevere*, Silvana Editoriale, 2010.

Gaulme, Dominique and Gaulme, François, *Power & style: A World History of Politics and Dress*. Flammarion, 2012.

Guardo, Lillian Langomarsino De, and Christina Garcia Pullés. *Y Ahora – Hablo Yo*, Editorial Sudamericana, 1996.

Gonthier, David F. Jr. and O'Brien, Timothy L, *The Films of Alan Parker, 1976–2003,* McFarland & Company, 2015. p.235.

Harbinson, W.A., *Evita: Saint Or Sinner?,* Boxtree Limited, 1997.

Hedges, Jill, *Evita: The Life of Eva Perón*, I.B. Tauris, 2017.

Hollander, Anne, *Sex and Suits: The Evolution of Modern Dress*, Alfred A. Knopf, 1994.

Jamandreu, Paco, *Evita fuera del balcón*, Caballo Negro, 2019.

Larson, Dolane J., *Evita's World: The Defining Years 1919–1947*, Create Space Independent Publishing Platform, 2017.

Lloyd Webber, Andrew and Rice, Tim, *Evita: The Legend of Eva Peron 1919–1952*, Book Club Associates, 1979.

Main, Mary, *Evita: The Woman with the Whip*, Corgi Books, 1977.

Martin, Richard and Koda, Harold, *Christian Dior*. The Metropolitan Museum of Art, New York, 1996.

McClendon, Emma, *Power Mode: The Force of Fashion,* Skira Editore, 2019.

Melo, Adrián, *Paco y Eva: las vidas paralelas de Evita Perón y Paquito Jamandreu: erotismo, política y diversidades sexuales en la literatura autobiográfica peronista*, Aurelia Rivera, 2020.

Ortiz, Alicia Dujovne, *Eva Perón: A Biography,* St Martin's Press, 1996.

Perón, Eva, *In my own words: Evita* (Laura Dail, Trans.), Mainstream Publishing Company Ltd, 1996.

Perón, Eva, *The Reason for my Life*, Asociación Museo Evita, 2016.

Perón, Juan Domingo, *Del poder al exilio*, Ediciones Argentinas, 1973.

Ricci, Stefania (Editor), *Museo Salvatore Ferragamo: Shoes and famous feet*, Leonardo Arte Books, 2000.

Rochas, Sophie, *Marcel Rochas: Designing French Glamour*, Flammarion, 2015.

Rogers, Ginger, *Ginger: My Story – Ginger Rogers*, Headline Book Publishing, 1991.

Sacquard de Bellefoche, Maud, *Eva Perón la Reine des Sans-chemises*, L'Imprimèrie Aubin, 1972.

Saulquin, Susana, *Historia de la moda Argentina: del miriñaque al diseño de autor*, Emecé Editores, 2006.

Saulquin, Susana, *Historia de la Moda Y El Diseño Argentino Desde 1776*, Diseño Editorial, 2019.

Saulquin, Susana, *Política de las apariencias: nueva significación del vestir en el contexto contemporáneo*, Paidós, 2014.

Seoane, María and Santa María, Victor, *Eva Perón: esa mujer*, Editorial Octubre, 2019.

Taylor, J.M., *Eva Perón: The Myths of a Woman*, University of Chicago Press, 1981.

Widmann-Miguel, Enrique, *Eva Perón En España*, Iberinfo, 2014. Available at: EVA PERÓN EN ESPAÑA_Enrique F. Widmann-Miguel_3ra Edición 2014 : IberInfo-Buenos Aires : Free Download, Borrow, and Streaming : Internet Archive

Young, Robb, *Power Dressing: First Ladies, Women Politicians & Fashion*, Merrell Publishers Limited, 2011.

Magazines and Newspapers

Careo
Cine Argentino
Damas y Damitas
Illustrated
In-Depth Magazine
La Settimana Incom Illustrata
Life Magazine
Maclean's Magazine
Picture Post
Radiolandia
Revista O Cruzeiro
Sintonía
The New York Times
Time
Tribuna Democrata

Articles and Theses

Castagnola, Gustavo, The Fashion of Politics: Argentina from the 1940s to the 2000s, *Österreichische Zeitschrift für Geschichtswissenschaften*, *15*(3), p.11. Available at: https://doi.org/10.25365/oezg-2004-15-3-2

Nijensohn, Daniel E., 'Prefrontal lobotomy on Evita was done for behavior/personality modification, not just for pain control' in *Neurosurgical Focus*, Volume 39: Issue 1 (July 2015): Infamous Neurological Injuries and Disease: Cases and Events of Historical, Political, Cultural, and Scientific Impact, 2015.

Walker, K. (2013). *Eva Perón and the Containment of Post-War New Womanhood: An Analysis of the International Press, 1945–1960* [Master's thesis, The University of Akron]. Available at: https://www.academia.edu/6045748/Eva_thesis_newest_draft

Web Links, Archives and Videos

All Musicals: https://www.allmusicals.com/lyrics/evita/theladysgotpotential.htm

BBC: http://news.bbc.co.uk/onthisday/hi/dates/stories/july/26/newsid_3660000/3660875.stm

Carroll, Rory, and Goni, Uri: *The Guardian*: https://www.theguardian.com/world/2007/oct/28/argentina.rorycarroll

Clarín: https://www.clarin.com/entremujeres/eva-peron-moda-estilo-aniversario_0_HJaMq3Yv7g.html

Daspin, Eileen: *The New York Times*: https://www.nytimes.com/1996/12/15/archives/cry-only-for-what-peron-really-wore.html

Duarte de Alvarez Rodríguez, Blanca: Evita Perón Historical Research Foundation: https://www.evitaperon.org/mens.htm

Hernndez, Y. Maria Teresa: The Independent: A prayer for Evita: Here's why many Argentinians are devoted to a first lady who died in 1952 | The Independent

Ibero-American Institute: https://digital.iai.spk-berlin.de/viewer/image/791361101/1/

Larson, Dolane: Evita Perón Historical Research Foundation: https://www.evitaperon.org/part2.htm

Life Magazine: Google Books: https://books.google.co.uk/books/about/LIFE.html?id=N0EEAAAAMBAJ&redir_esc=y

Metha, Shirin: Queen Rania Al Abdullah: https://www.queenrania.jo/en/media/news/monday-january-1-2007-shirin-mehta-verve-magazine-0

Miller, Scott: New Line Theatre: https://newlinetheatre.com/evitachapter.html

Nix, Michelle: YouTube: https://www.youtube.com/watch?v=aEuWG8_XW8Y

Oloixarac, Pola: *The New York Times*: https://www.nytimes.com/2019/12/05/opinion/argentina-cristina-fernandez-de-kirchner.html

Pengelly, Martin: *The Guardian*: https://www.theguardian.com/us-news/2019/jul/07/donald-trump-alexandria-ocasio-cortez-evita-american-carnage

Perón, Eva: Iowa State University: https://awpc.cattcenter.iastate.edu/2018/01/09/renunciation-of-the-vice-presidency-of-argentina-aug-31-1951/

Perón, Eva: Iowa State University: https://awpc.cattcenter.iastate.edu/2017/10/11/final-speech-october-17-1951/

Peterson, Beatrice: ABC News: https://abcnews.go.com/Politics/trump-loves-evita-presidency/story?id=59350378

Pictorial Gems: Ebay: https://www.ebay.co.uk/itm/333168129874

Sarlo, Beatriz: A representação de Eva: https://piaui.folha.uol.com.br/materia/a-representacao-de-eva/

Schild, Darcy: *Business Insider*: https://www.businessinsider.com/aoc-alexandria-ocasio-cortez-style-fashion-statements-2020-11

Secreteria de Cultura: https://www.cultura.gob.ar/annemarie-heinrich-la-fotografa-de-evita-8997/

Smith, David: *The Guardian*: https://www.theguardian.com/us-news/2019/mar/31/alexandria-ocasio-cortez-aoc-republicans-trump

Sturcke, James: *The Guardian*: https://www.theguardian.com/world/2007/oct/29/argentina.jamessturcke

The Guardian: https://www.theguardian.com/world/2012/jul/26/eva-peron-evita-argentina-banknotes

The Musical Lyrics: https://themusicallyrics.com/e/293-evita-the-musical-lyrics/2497-you-must-love-me-lyrics.html

The National Archives: https://www.nationalarchives.gov.uk/

The Royal Archives: https://www.royal.uk/the-royal-archives

The West Australian: https://thewest.com.au/lifestyle/fashion/designer-pays-homage-to-evita-ng-ya-207798

Time: https://web.archive.org/web/20011221053805/http:/www.time.com/time/magazine/1997/int/970120/cinema.the_woman.html

Time: https://web.archive.org/web/20090616110842/http:/www.time.com/time/magazine/article/0,9171,888638,00.html

Time: https://time.com/archive/6620893/argentina-cinderellas-double/

Watson, Katy: BBC News: https://www.bbc.co.uk/news/world-latin-america-68601194

Zmirak, John: *The Stream*: https://stream.org/the-democrats-new-evita-peron-needs-to-spend-3-months-in-venezuela/

Endnotes

Introduction

1. *Time* (1947), 'Little Eva' 14 July, p.24.
2. Perón, Eva, *The Reason for my Life*, Asociación Museo Evita, 2016. p.3–5.

Chapter 1

1. *La Razón de mi vida*, Ediciones Asociación Museo Evita, Buenos Aires, 2016. p.275.
2. Ibid. p.13.
3. Ibid. p.22.
4. Duarte de Alvarez Rodríguez, Blanca, (1997). Blanca Duarte: 'Our True Life'. Available at: Objectives Evita Perón Historical Research Foundation (Accessed: 22 March 2023).
5. *La Razón de mi vida*, Ediciones Asociación Museo Evita, Buenos Aires, 2016. p.243.
6. Duarte de Alvarez Rodríguez, Blanca, (1997). Blanca Duarte: 'Our True Life'. Available at: Objectives Evita Perón Historical Research Foundation (Accessed: 22 March 2023).
7. Eva y la moda: una mujer con sello propio (2012). Available at: Eva y la moda: una mujer con sello propio (clarin.com) (Accessed: 17 November 2023).

Chapter 2

1. Las inocentes (1936001800). Available at: https://digital.iai.spk-berlin.de/viewer/image/791361101/1/ (Accessed: 17 June 2023).
2. Annemarie Heinrich y sus retratos de Evita (2020). Available at: Annemarie Heinrich and her portraits of Evita | Culture (cultura.gob.ar) (Accessed: 4 June 2023).

3. Fraser, Nicholas and Navarro, Marysa, *Evita: The Real Lives of Eva Perón,* Carlton Publishing Group, 2003. p.25-26.
4. Aringoli, Guillermo Enrique D'Arino, *Evita en Europa: Un viaje iniciático. La construcción del mito*, Caligrama, 2018. p.23.
5. Miller, Scott, (2010). Available at: Inside Evita by Scott Miller (newlinetheatre.com) (Accessed: 2 January 2024).
6. Josephs, Ray, 'She Dictates to the Dictator', *Maclean's Magazine*, December 15, 1948. p.17.

Chapter 3

1. Aringoli, Guillermo Enrique D'Arino, *Evita en Europa: Un viaje iniciático. La construcción del mito*, Caligrama, 2018. p.35
2. Francisco Vicente 'Paco' Jamandreu (1925–1995) was an Argentine fashion designer, costume designer for film, and actor. Paco grew up between his aristocratic paternal grandmother in Spain, and his provincial maternal grandmother in Argentina. Having to change schools and clothing every six months turned Paco into something of a loner who discovered a creative outlet through fashion. His first big break came as a costume designer for actress Zully Moreno. Eva Perón would become his most famous client.
3. Jamandreu's celebrity anecdotes, largely narrated by himself, are often tricky to corroborate.
4. Balmaceda, Daniel, *Qué tenían puesto: La moda en la historia argentina*, Sudamericana, 2018.
5. Larson, Dolane J., *Evita's World: The Defining Years 1919–1947.* Create Space Independent Publishing Platform, 2017. p.103.
6. Aringoli, Guillermo Enrique D'Arino, *Evita en Europa: Un viaje iniciático. La construcción del mito*, Caligrama, 2018. p.42.
7. Eva must also have valued the dress as it is the only personal dress from her life as an actress to have survived in the Museo Evita collection.
8. This Christmas tradition would be continued through the Eva Perón Foundation.
9. Possibly designed by costumier Thomas Hay. Now in the collection of the Museo Evita.

10. *Radiolandia*, 7 April 1945.
11. *Time*, June 1945.
12. Eva never forgot this injustice and would later take revenge by having the state buy the station from Yankelevich in 1947.
13. Perón, Eva, *The Reason for my Life*, Asociación Museo Evita, 2016. p.42
14. Melo, Adrián, *Paco y Eva: las vidas paralelas de Evita Perón y Paquito Jamandreu: erotismo, política y diversidades sexuales en la literatura autobiográfica peronista*, Aurelia Rivera, 2020. p.72.
15. Josephs, Ray, 'She Dictates to the Dictator', *Maclean's Magazine*, 15 December 1948. p.40.

Chapter 4

1. Young, Robb, *Power Dressing: First Ladies, Women Politicians & Fashion*, Merrell Publishers Limited, 2011. p.17–19.
2. Rogers, Ginger, *Ginger: My Story – Ginger Rogers*, Headline Book Publishing, 1991. p.285.
3. Anthony, Carl Sferrazza, *Why They Wore It: The Politics & Pop Culture of First Ladies' Fashion*, The Richard Nixon Foundation, 2018.
4. The house of Henriette was founded in 1918 by the five Schwartz sisters, daughters of a Romanian furrier. Inspired by a meeting between the elder sister Sarina and a commission agent who travelled between Paris and Argentina selling French designs; the house became known for its copies of Parisian couture. At its peak, the house operated with 200 employees who dressed the cream of Argentine society.
5. Paula Naletoff arrived in Buenos Aires from Belgrade in 1928, where she had run her own fashion house. She opened her business, originally from her apartment, in 1934, which became known for its spectacular evening dresses. Paula Naletoff passed away in 1984. The Museo Evita care for more garments by Paula Naletoff than by any other designers.
6. Saulquin, Susana, *Historia de la moda Argentina: del miriñaque al diseño de autor, Emecé Editores*, 2006. p.126.

7. Eva Perón has not been the only famous woman to be dismissed from a fashion boutique. When Lady Diana Spencer was looking for an outfit to wear for the photoshoot to announce her engagement to Prince Charles, she visited the Bellville Sassoon boutique. Not recognising the future Princess of Wales, a saleslady advised the young woman to try shopping somewhere more affordable.
8. Bernarda Noci de Meneses had been the owner of a distinguished fashion house in Barcelona until she was hired as director of Paquin by the brand's public relations director, Ana de Pombo, in 1937. Upon leaving Paquin in 1939, de Meneses founded the house of Bernarda that opened in September 1940 and became famous as one of the most important names in Argentine haute couture.
9. Saulquin, Susana, *Historia de la moda Argentina: del miriñaque al diseño de autor*, Emecé Editores, 2006. p.126.
10. Saulquin, Susana, *Política de las apariencias: nueva significación del vestir en el contexto contemporáneo*, Paidós, 2014. p.146.
11. Ortiz, Alicia Dujovne, *Eva Perón: A Biography, St Martin's Press*, 1996. p.157.
12. André Perugia (1893–1977) began his shoe-making apprenticeship in his father's workshop in Nice, before his shoes came to the attention of master couturier Paul Poiret in 1914. The outbreak of the First World War put a hold on Perugia's career as he was requisitioned to work in an aircraft factory. The engineering techniques that he learnt transformed his ideas about the development of shoe design and led to the creation of a steel alloy heel. He established his own shop on the rue du Faubourg Saint-Honoré in 1921, where he became known for his use of exotic materials, including antelope and horsehair. Perugia collaborated with designers ranging from the avant-garde Elsa Schiaparelli to the more conservative Jacques Fath, and his shoes were worn by clients including Rita Hayworth and Josephine Baker.
13. Perón, Eva, *The Reason for my Life*, Asociación Museo Evita, 2016. p.166.
14. Elfriede Isabel Catalina Constancia Ernst (1924–2000) was born in Cologne. Her parents emigrated to Uruguay in 1926 before settling in Argentina. Ernst was forced to abandon her rising political career

upon discovering that she was pregnant as a result of her affair with Colonel Mercante (who was already the father of two children with his wife Elena Caporale).

15. Carlson, Marifran, ¡Feminismo!: The Woman's Movement in Argentina from its Beginnings to Eva Perón, Chicago Review Press, 2005. p.189.
16. Perón, Eva, The Reason for my Life, Asociación Museo Evita, 2016. p.265.
17. Ibid. p.267.
18. Ibid. p.104.
19. Perón, Eva, *The Reason for my Life*, Asociación Museo Evita, 2016. p.86–87.
20. Fraser, Nicholas and Navarro, Marysa, Evita: The Real Lives of Eva Perón, Carlton Publishing Group, 2003. p.82.
21. The Sociedad de Beneficencia de Buenos Aires was created in 1823 in order to transfer authority for social work from the Catholic church to the new state institution, after Argentine independence. The Sociedad was disbanded by President Perón in 1947.
22. The Store of Delights.
23. These items all exist in the Museo Evita collection.
24. Aringoli, Guillermo Enrique D'Arino, Evita en Europa: Un viaje iniciático. La construcción del mito, Caligrama, 2018. p.74.
25. The National Archives of the UK (TNA): FO 118/755: Political: Argentine internal.
26. Neville, Robert, *How Evita Helps Run Argentina*, *Life Magazine* 11 December 1950. p.74.
27. Lloyd Webber, Andrew and Rice, Tim, *Evita: The Legend of Eva Peron 1919–1952*, Book Club Associates, 1979. p.68.

Chapter 5

1. Mitchell, David, 'The Amazing Life of Eva Perón', *Picture Post*, 5 July 1952. p.19.
2. Saulquin, Susana, *Política de las apariencias: nueva significación del vestir en el contexto contemporáneo*, Paidós, 2014. p.147.

3. Reported in the *Tribuna Democrata*, 30 April 1947. p.2.
4. Ana de Pombo (1900–1985) was a Spanish designer and businesswoman. She founded her own fashion house, Chez Elviana, in Paris in 1928, but sold it to become personal secretary to Gabrielle 'Coco' Chanel. de Pombo left Chanel due to professional differences and was hired by Jeanna Paquin to manage her fashion houses in London, Paris and Buenos Aires. It was in Buenos Aires after the war that de Pombo would found her namesake fashion house, which became famous for the haute couture designs she created for Eva Perón and for the silver screen.
5. Aringoli, Guillermo Enrique D'Arino, *Evita en Europa: Un viaje iniciático. La construcción del mito*, Caligrama, 2018. p.87.
6. Ibid. p.95.
7. Mitchell, David, *The Amazing Life of Eva Perón*, Picture Post, July 5, 1952. p.19.
8. Since its creation in 1815, only 72,398 people have received the Order. (de Ceballos-Escalera y Gila, Alfonso (2015). *La Real y Americana Orden de Isabel La Catolica*. Boletin Oficial del Estado. p.186.)
9. After President Perón was overthrown in 1955, the costumes were seized alongside Eva's other clothes and stored in the Municipal Bank in Buenos Aires. When protests broke out about the military government's proposal to auction the costumes in 1966, a decree was signed to transfer ownership of the collection of provincial costumes to the Museo de Arte Español Enrique Larreta.
10. Guardo, Lillian Langomarsino De, and Christina Garcia Pullés. Y Ahora – Hablo Yo, Editorial Sudamericana, 1996. p.133.
11. Widmann-Miguel, Enrique, Eva Perón En España, Iberfino, 2014. p.80-82. Available at: EVA PERÓN EN ESPAÑA_Enrique F. Widmann-Miguel_3ra Edición 2014 : IberInfo-Buenos Aires : Free Download, Borrow, and Streaming : Internet Archive. (Accessed 24 January 2024).
12. Widmann-Miguel, Enrique, *Eva Perón En España*, Iberfino, 2014. p.173-175. Available at: EVA PERÓN EN ESPAÑA_Enrique F. Widmann-Miguel_3ra Edición 2014 : IberInfo-Buenos Aires : Free

Download, Borrow, and Streaming : Internet Archive. (Accessed 24 January 2024).

13. *Time* (1947) 'Dashing Blonde', 23 June, p.36.
14. Ibid.
15. Widmann-Miguel, Enrique, Eva Perón En España, Iberfino, 2014. pp.195–6. Available at: EVA PERÓN EN ESPAÑA_Enrique F. Widmann-Miguel_3ra Edición 2014 : IberInfo-Buenos Aires : Free Download, Borrow, and Streaming : Internet Archive. (Accessed 24 January 2024).
16. Italian fashion designer Fernanda Gattinoni (1906–2002) was born in the Lombardy region. She started her career working for Edward Molyneux, and even turned down a job at Chanel. She returned to Italy in 1930, where she began working for Domenico Ventura's Milanese fashion house. She would find international success with her own self-named atelier in the 1950s, that became popular with the international jet set. The costumes she designed for King Vidor's epic production of War & Peace, earned a nomination for the 1957 Academy Award for Best Costume Design.
17. Salvatore Ferragamo (1898–1960) begun his shoemaking apprentice in his hometown of Bonito, where he opened a small shop in his parent's home. Like many other young Italian men in the early twentieth century, he emigrated in search of the American dream. America opened his eyes to the benefits of mechanised shoe production but also highlighted how the finished shoe would never reach the high standards of Ferragamo's hand-crafted artisan designs. After a stint running his exclusive business in California, that became known as the 'shoe shop to the stars' due to his Hollywood clients, he began studying the anatomy of the foot at the University of Southern California to better understand how to support a woman's body weight comfortably in his shoes. Ferragamo moved back to Italy in 1927 where he was able to combine American techniques of mass production with Italian craftsmanship.
18. Brin, Irene, *De lai si vestono attrici e ambasciatrici*, La Settimana Incom Illustrata, 9 June 1951.
19. Ferragamo, Salvatore, *Shoemaker of Dreams: The Autobiography of Salvatore Ferragamo*, George G. Harrap & Co. Ltd.,1957. pp.217–8.

20. Ricci, Stefania (ed.), *Museo Salvatore Ferragamo: Shoes and famous feet*, Leonardo Arte Books, 2000. p.126.
21. The relationship between the two countries was strong, with exports of Argentine beef having played a significant role in feeding the British population during the war.
22. Dixon, Pierson, Letter from Pierson Dixon to Sir Alan Lascelles. Letter. 4 June 1947. RA PS/PSO/GVI/PS/MAIN/7353. The Royal Archives, Windsor Castle, UK.
23. *Sunday Pictorial.*
24. Charles, Sir Noel, Telegram from Sir Noel Charles to the Foreign Office. Telegram. 5 July 1947. RA PS/PSO/GVI/PS/MAIN/7353. The Royal Archives, Windsor Castle, UK.
25. Eva would be featured on the cover of *Time Magazine* again in 1951, this time with President Juan Perón.
26. *Time* (1947) 'Little Eva', 14 July, p.22.
27. Ibid.
28. Main, Mary, *Evita: The Woman with the Whip*, Corgi Books, 1977. pp.120–1.
29. Maison de l'Amerique Latine, Careo, July 1962, p.12.
30. Sacquard de Bellefoche, Maud, *Eva Perón la Reine des Sans-chemises*, L'Imprimèrie Aubin, 1972. pp.120–1.
31. Christian Dior (1905–1957) came to prominence with his first collection that debuted in 1947, heralding a return to feminine silhouettes. The editor-in-chief of *Harper's Bazaar*, Carmel Snow, gave the Corolle collection its now ubiquitous name when she told Dior: 'It's quite a revelation dear Christian … Your dresses have such a new look.' Dior helped to reestablish Paris as the centre of post-war fashion and pioneered the use of product licensing that made Dior a household name.
32. Jacques Fath (1912–1954) was called the 'couturier's couturier'. Fashion ran in his family and his great-grandmother had worked as a couturière to Empress Eugénie of France. He launched his first collection in 1937, and expanded his brand with his wife, the former model, Geneviève Boucher. His innovative designs made him a household name along with the other post-war haute couture designers, Christian Dior and

Pierre Balmain. His career, and the future of his fashion house, was cut shut upon his death from leukaemia.

33. Benaim, Laurence, *Women in Dior: Portraits of Elegance*, Rizzoli International Publications Inc., 2016. p.88.
34. *Time* (1947) 'La Belle Blonde', 4 August, p.26.
35. 'Eyewitness of Evita's visit to Paris' *In-Depth Magazine* N° 60, July-August 1988, Buenos Aires, p.17.
36. The book was first published in September 1951 by Ediciones Peuser with an initial print run of 300,000 copies.
37. Mitchell, David, *The Amazing Life of Eva Perón*, Picture Post, July 5, 1952. p.20.
38. *Time* (1947) 'Little Eva'. 14 July, p.22.

Chapter 6

1. Josephs, Ray, *She Dictates to the Dictator*, Maclean's Magazine, December 15, 1948. p.17.
2. Young, Robb, *Power Dressing: First Ladies, Women Politicians & Fashion*, Merrell Publishers Limited, 2011. p.63.
3. Shirin, Metha, *In Interview with Verve Magazine, Queen Rania Talks about Visit to India* (2007). Available at: In Interview with Verve Magazine, Queen Rania Talks about Visit to India | Queen Rania (Accessed: 4 February 2024).
4. Perón, Eva, *The Reason for my Life*, Asociación Museo Evita, 2016. p.311.
5. Mitchell, David, *The Amazing Life of Eva Perón*, Picture Post, July 5, 1952. p.19.
6. Young, Robb, Power Dressing: First Ladies, Women Politicians & Fashion, Merrell Publishers Limited, 2011. p.8.
7. The House of Dior kept a mannequin with Eva's exact measurements (taken during her visit to Paris) in the atelier that eliminated the need for Eva to travel for fittings.
8. Neville, Robert, *How Evita Helps Run Argentina*, *Life Magazine* 11 December 1950. p.82.
9. Saulquin, Susana, *Historia de la moda Argentina: del miriñaque al diseño de autor*, Emecé Editores, 2006. p.129.

10. Neville, Robert, 'How Evita Helps Run Argentina', *Life Magazine* 11 December 1950. p.82.
11. Cosgrove, Charles H.; Yeo, Khiok-Khng; Weiss, Herold B., *Cross-Cultural Paul: Journeys to Others, Journeys to Ourselves*, W.B. Eerdmans Publishing Company, 2005. p.45.
12. Benjamin, Walter, *The Work of Art in the Age of Mechanical Reproduction*, Penguin, 2008.
13. Translates loosely to 'easy', referring to Eva's dubious past.
14. Sarlo, Beatriz, 'A representação de Eva' (2012). Available at: A representação de Eva – revista piauí (uol.com.br) (Accessed: 12 December 2023).
15. Mitchell, David, *The Amazing Life of Eva Perón*, Picture Post, July 5, 1952. p.18.
16. *Fundacion Eva Perón, Estatutos*, Buenos Aires, 1955. pp.1-2.
17. Perón, Eva, *The Reason for my Life*, Asociación Museo Evita, 2016. p.184.
18. Castiñeira de Dios, José Maria, interviewed by Nicholas Fraser and Marysa Navarro, *Evita: The Real Lives of Vea Perón*, Carlton Publishing Group, 2003. p.127.
19. Seen from above, the street layout of which bares an uncanny resemblance to the silhouette of Eva Perón.
20. Perón, Eva, *The Reason for my Life*, Asociación Museo Evita, 2016. p.13-14
21. An Argentinean expression roughly translating as 'greasy' or 'fatties'.
22. Perón, Eva, *In my own words: Evita* (Laura Dail, Trans.), Mainstream Publishing Company Ltd, 1996. p.90.
23. Neville, Robert, 'How Evita Helps Run Argentina', *Life Magazine*, 11 December 1950. p.81.
24. Perón, Eva, *The Reason for my Life*, Asociación Museo Evita, 2016. p.88.
25. Neville, Robert, 'How Evita Helps Run Argentina', *Life Magazine* 11 December, 1950. p.74.
26. Dos Passos, John, 'to Eva', *Life Magazine* 11 April, 1949. p.31.
27. Hollander, Anne, *Sex and Suits: The Evolution of Modern Dress*, Alfred A. Knopf, 1994. p.5.
28. Perón, Eva, *The Reason for my Life*, Asociación Museo Evita, 2016. p.83.

29. Josephs, Ray, 'She Dictates to the Dictator', *Maclean's Magazine*, 15 December 1948. p.37.

Chapter 7

1. The National Archives of the UK (TNA): FO 371/81237: Health of Eva Perón: Code AA file 1791.
2. Ibid.
3. Ibid.
4. *Illustrated* (1950) 'Private Life of Fairy Eva', 23 September, p.9.
5. Ortiz, Alicia Dujovne, *Eva Perón: A Biography,* St Martin's Press, 1996. p.250.
6. The National Archives of the UK (TNA): FO 371/81247: Publication on 13 Oct 1950 by Ministry of Labour of resolution enjoining all employers to retain two days wages of each employee as a contribution to the Eva Perón Fund: Code AA file 2187.
7. Cowles, Fleur, *Bloody Precedent: The Peron Story*, Frederick Muller Ltd, 1952. p.164.
8. 'Fleur's Flair' (1949). Available at: Fleur's Flair – *TIME* (archive.org) (Accessed: 12 September 2023).
9. Cowles, Fleur, *Bloody Precedent: The Peron Story*, Frederick Muller Ltd, 1952. p.165.
10. Ibid. p.176
11. Cowles, Fleur, *Bloody Precedent: The Peron Story*, Frederick Muller Ltd, 1952. p.185.
12. 'Not a Woman's Woman' (1952). Available at: ARGENTINA: Not a Woman's Woman | TIME (Accessed: 17 November 2023).
13. *Life Magazine* (1950) 'Eva Perón: A First Look at the Private Life of a Controversial First Lady', 11 December, p.70–1.
14. Christian Dior Spring-Summer 1950 *Verticale* line haute couture collection.
15. Neville, Robert, *How Evita Helps Run Argentina*, Life Magazine: December 11, 1950. p.82.
16. Fontaine, Joan, *No Bed of Roses*, William Morrow and Company, 1978. p.207.
17. Ibid.

18. Ibid.
19. Eva would later be selected to represent the year 1946 for *Time* magazine's 100 'Women of the Year'.
20. Main, Mary, *Evita: The Woman with the Whip*, Corgi Books, 1977. p.10.
21. French designer Marcel Rochas (1902–1955) founded his eponymous fashion house in 1925. His pervading use of black and white, ribbons, and Chantilly lace can all be seen in a surviving 1951 cocktail ensemble that belonged to Eva Perón and is now in the care of the Museo de la Mode, Chile.
22. The Dior evening dress and coat, and the Rochas dress, all survive in the Museo Evita.
23. Rochas, Sophie, Marcel Rochas: *Designing French Glamour*, Flammarion, 2015. p.108
24. Perón, Maria Eva, *Renunciation of the vice presidency* (1951). Available at: Renunciation of the vice presidency of Argentina – Aug. 31, 1951 | Archives of Women's Political Communication (iastate.edu) (Accessed: 13 September 2023).
25. Father Benitzez's memoir of Eva, *Careo*, July 1964. p.17.
26. Perón, Maria Eva, *Speech to the Descamisados* (1951). Available at: Speech to the Descamisados – Oct. 17, 1951 | Archives of Women's Political Communication (iastate.edu) (Accessed: 13 September 2023).
27. Aringoli, Guillermo Enrique D'Arino, *Evita en Europa: Un viaje iniciático. La construcción del* mito, Caligrama, 2018. p.387.

Chapter 8

1. '1952 French Boxer George Carpentier With Argentine President And Eva Peron'. Available at: 1952 French Boxer George Carpentier With Argentine President And Eva Peron | eBay (Accessed: 22 March 2024).
2. Perón, Juan Domingo, Del poder al exilio, Ediciones Argentinas, 1973. p.61.
3. A Dior evening ensemble, consisting of a flamenco-inspired red silk embroidered taffeta dress with a black silk faille bolero, purchased

by Eva from the 1952 collection is now part of the MET Museum collection in New York.

4. The Museo Evita have several garments in their collection that show signs of having been taken in during the final years of Eva's life. A dress also exists in pieces that may have been taken apart to be made smaller but not completed before the Eva's death.
5. Ortiz, Alicia Dujovne, *Eva Perón: A Biography*, St Martin's Press, 1996. p.276
6. Perón, Juan Domingo, Del poder al exilio, Ediciones Argentinas, 1973. p.62.
7. 25 June 1952.
8. It is believed that Eva weighed only 36 kg by June 1952.
9. After the 1955 coup that overthrew President Perón, Paco Jamendreu's friendship with the Peróns led to him emigrating to Brazil. He returned to Argentina in the 1960s and resumed his career until his death from a heart attack in 1995.
10. Nijensohn, Daniel E., 'Prefrontal lobotomy on Evita was done for behavior/personality modification, not just for pain control' in *Neurosurgical Focus*, Volume 39: Issue 1 (July 2015): Infamous Neurological Injuries and Disease: Cases and Events of Historical, Political, Cultural, and Scientific Impact, 2015.
11. Father Benitzez' memoir of Eva, *Careo*, July 1964. p.19
12. Saulquin, Susana, *Política de las apariencias: nueva significación del vestir en el contexto contemporáneo*, Paidós, 2014. p.152.
13. Benaim, Laurence, *Women in Dior: Portraits of Elegance*, Rizzoli International Publications Inc., 2016. p.88.
14. *Life Ma*gazine (1952) 'Grief for Eva Enshrouds Argentina', 11 August, p.52.
15. 1952: Eva Perón Dies. Available at: BBC ON THIS DAY | 26 | 1952: Eva Perón dies (Accessed: 2 September 2023).
16. *Life Magazine* (1952) 'Life on the Newsfronts of the World', 4 August, p.32.
17. The shroud was put up for sale at Christie's auction house by a former aide to Juan Perón in 2004. It sold for $159,300, more than three times its estimate.

Chapter 9

1. Mitchell, David, 'The Amazing Life of Eva Perón', *Picture Post*, 5 July, 1952. p.15.
2. Harbinson, W.A., *Evita: Saint Or Sinner?*, Boxtree Limited, 1997. p.73.
3. The Museo Evita has a dress with scissor damage to the centre back of the skirt that they have chosen not to conserve. This dress has been exhibited with the damage displayed as they believe it is now part of the history of the dress.
4. Hedges, Jill, *Evita: The Life of Eva Perón*, I.B. Tauris, 2017. p.225.
5. *Revista O Cruzeiro* (1956), 'Eva's Treasure', 7 January.
6. Walker, K. (2013). Eva Perón and the Containment of Post-War New Womanhood: An Analysis of the International Press, 1945–1960 [Master's thesis, The University of Akron]. p.2. Available at: https://www.academia.edu/6045748/Eva_thesis_newest_draft
7. Martínez, Tomás Eloy, 'The Woman Behind the Fantasy: Prostitute, Fascist, Profligate – Eva Perón Was Much Maligned, Mostly Unfairly', *Time* Vol. 149: No. 3, January 20, 1997. Available at: THE WOMAN BEHIND THE FANTASY (archive.org) (Accessed: 15 March 2023).
8. Castagnola, Gustavo, 'The Fashion of Politics: Argentina from the 1940s to the 2000s', *Österreichische Zeitschrift für Geschichtswissenschaften*, *15*(3), p.11. Available at: https://doi.org/10.25365/oezg-2004-15-3-2 (Accessed 20 January 2024).
9. Evita Fashion Inspires Argentina (2010). Available at: https://thewest.com.au/lifestyle/fashion/designer-pays-homage-to-evita-ng-ya-207798 (Accessed: 19 January 2023).
10. *Time* (1953) 'Cinderella's Double', Available at: ARGENTINA: Cinderella's Double | TIME (Accessed: 25 September 2023).
11. Fraser, Nicholas and Navarro, Marysa, *Evita: The Real Lives of Eva Perón,* Carlton Publishing Group, 2003. p.193
12. Michael, Mick St, *Madonna talking: Madonna in Her Own Words*, Omnibus Press, 2004. p.67.
13. Personal correspondence with Ludovica Barabino of the Fondazione Ferragamo.

14. Daspin, Eileen, 'Cry Only for What Perón Really Wore', *The New York Times* (1996). Available at: Cry Only for What Perón Really Wore – The New York Times (nytimes.com) (Accessed: 19 January 2023).
15. Ibid.
16. Stronger, Karol, 'Dior and Evita again paired in union of style and spirit', *The New York Times*, 21 September, 2005.
17. Gonthier, David F. Jr. and O'Brien, Timothy L., *The Films of Alan Parker, 1976–2003*, McFarland & Company, 2015. p.235.
18. Lloyd Webber, Andrew and Rice, Tim, *Evita: The Legend of Eva Peron 1919–1952*, Book Club Associates, 1979. p.109.

Chapter 10

1. 'The President Wore Pearls', *The Simpsons* (Season 15, episode 3 – 2003).
2. Perón, Eva, *The Reason for my Life*, Asociación Museo Evita, 2016. p.95.
3. Watson, Katy, *Irina Karamanos and the first ladies forging their own path* (2024). Available at: Irina Karamanos and the first ladies forging their own path – BBC News (Accessed: 25 April 2024).
4. Ibid.
5. *Life Magazine* (1952) 'Women of Chile Get Their Man', 15 September, p.45.
6. Ibid.
7. Isabel Martínez de Perón (born 4 February 1931) was a former dancer who met Juan Perón during his exile in Panama. The couple married in Spain in 1961. Isabel undertook a number of trips to Argentina in the 1960s and 1970s to build support for Perón's political return.
8. Carroll, Rory, and Goni, Uki, *First Lady of Argentina ready to be the new Evita* (2007). Available at: First Lady of Argentina ready to be the new Evita | World news | The Guardian (Accessed: 20 April 2024).
9. Sturcke, James, *The art of the possible* (2007). Available at: The art of the possible | World news | The Guardian (Accessed: 20 April 2024).
10. Ibid.

11. Oloixarac, Pola, 'A New Evita Rises in Argentina' (2019). Available at: Opinion | A New Evita Rises in Argentina – The New York Times (nytimes.com) (Accessed: 15 April 2024).
12. 'Evita fits the bill – Eva Perón to become first woman on Argentinian banknotes' (2012). Available at: Evita fits the bill – Eva Perón to become first woman on Argentinian banknotes | Eva Perón | The Guardian (Accessed: 15 April 2024).
13. Nix, Michelle, 'Bless Her Heart' (2019). Available at: Michele Nix for Congress – 'Bless Her Heart' (youtube.com) (Accessed: 6 May 2024).
14. Zmirak, John, 'The Democrats' New Evita Perón Needs to Spend 3 Months in Venezuela' (2018). Available at: The Democrats' New Evita Perón Needs to Spend 3 Months in Venezuela – The Stream (Accessed: 6 May 2024).
15. Smith, David, '"AOC TMZ": why Republicans obsess over Alexandria Ocasio-Cortez' (2019). Available at: 'AOC TMZ': why Republicans obsess over Alexandria Ocasio-Cortez | Alexandria Ocasio-Cortez | The Guardian (Accessed: 7 May 2024).
16. Pengelly, Martin, 'Trump calls Ocasio-Cortez "Evita" in new book American Carnage' (2019). Available at: Trump calls Ocasio-Cortez 'Evita' in new book American Carnage | Alexandria Ocasio-Cortez | The Guardian (Accessed: 6 May 2024).
17. Ibid.
18. Alexandria Ocasio-Cortez, Twitter, 7 July 2019. (Accessed: 5 May 2024).
19. Peterson, Beatrice, 'Why Trump loves 'Evita,' and what it says about his presidency'. Available at: Why Trump loves 'Evita,' and what it says about his presidency – ABC News (go.com) (Accessed: 5 May 2024).
20. Schild, Darcy, 'Alexandria Ocasio-Cortez is changing the dress code of politics' (2020). Available at: How AOC Embraces Power-Dressing and Proves Fashion Can Be Political (businessinsider.com) (Accessed: 7 May 2024).
21. Alexandria Ocasio-Cortez, Twitter, 4 January 2019. (Accessed: 5 May 2024).

22. Alexandria Ocasio-Cortez, Instagram, 14 September 2021. (Accessed: 5 May 2024).
23. 'Evita fits the bill – Eva Perón to become first woman on Argentinian banknotes' (2012). Available at: Evita fits the bill – Eva Perón to become first woman on Argentinian banknotes | Eva Perón | The Guardian (Accessed: 15 April 2024).

Epilogue

1. *Illustrated* (1950) 'Private Life of Fairy Eva' 23 September, p.10.
2. Hernndez, Y. Maria Teresa, A prayer for Evita: Here's why many Argentinians are devoted to a first lady who died in 1952. Available at: A prayer for Evita: Here's why many Argentinians are devoted to a first lady who died in 1952 | The Independent (Accessed: 3 March 2024).
3. Anthony, Carl Sferrazza, *Why They Wore It: The Politics & Pop Culture of First Ladies' Fashion*, The Richard Nixon Foundation, 2018. p.3.
4. Young, Robb, *Power Dressing: First Ladies, Women Politicians & Fashion*, Merrell Publishers Limited, 2011. p.153.
5. Perón, Eva, *The Reason for my Life*, Asociación Museo Evita, 2016. p.90-91.
6. Neville, Robert, 'How Evita Helps Run Argentina', *Life Magazine*, 11 December 1950. p.78.
7. Perón, Eva, The Reason for my Life, Asociación Museo Evita, 2016.p.95.

Index